D0938782

Death Penalty

Other Books in the Current Controversies Series

Death Penalty

Noël Merino, Book Editor

GREENHAVEN PRESS
A part of Gale, Cengage Learning

GALE
CENGAGE Learning·

Farmington Hills, Mich • San Francisco • New York • Waterville, Maine
Meriden, Conn • Mason, Ohio • Chicago

Mohawk Valley Community College Library

GALE
CENGAGE Learning

Patricia Coryell, *Vice President & Publisher, New Products & GVRL*
Douglas Dentino, *Manager, New Products*
Judy Galens, *Acquisitions Editor*

© 2015 Greenhaven Press, a part of Gale, Cengage Learning

WCN: 01-100-101

Gale and Greenhaven Press are registered trademarks used herein under license.

For more information, contact:
Greenhaven Press
27500 Drake Rd.
Farmington Hills, MI 48331-3535
Or you can visit our Internet site at gale.cengage.com

ALL RIGHTS RESERVED.
No part of this work covered by the copyright herein may be reproduced, transmitted, stored, or used in any form or by any means graphic, electronic, or mechanical, including but not limited to photocopying, recording, scanning, digitizing, taping, Web distribution, information networks, or information storage and retrieval systems, except as permitted under Section 107 or 108 of the 1976 United States Copyright Act, without the prior written permission of the publisher.

For product information and technology assistance, contact us at

Gale Customer Support, 1-800-877-4253
For permission to use material from this text or product, submit all requests online at www.cengage.com/permissions

Further permissions questions can be emailed to permissionrequest@cengage.com

Articles in Greenhaven Press anthologies are often edited for length to meet page requirements. In addition, original titles of these works are changed to clearly present the main thesis and to explicitly indicate the author's opinion. Every effort is made to ensure that Greenhaven Press accurately reflects the original intent of the authors. Every effort has been made to trace the owners of copyrighted material.

Cover image copyright © Scott Olson/Hulton Archive/Getty Images.

LIBRARY OF CONGRESS CATALOGING-IN-PUBLICATION DATA

Death penalty / Noël Merino, book editor.
    pages cm. -- (Current controversies)
Includes bibliographical references and index.
ISBN 978-0-7377-7213-5 (hardcover) -- ISBN 978-0-7377-7214-2 (pbk.)
1. Capital punishment--United States. I. Merino, Noël.
HV8699.U5D3562 2015
364.660973--dc23
                                                                        2014039597

Printed in Mexico
1 2 3 4 5 6 7 19 18 17 16 15

HV
8699
.U5
D3562
2015

Contents

Chapter 3: Is the Death Penalty Applied Fairly?

Most prisoners with death sentences are male and just over half are white, and many end up with their sentence commuted or overturned. Of the more than eight thousand inmates sentenced to death from 1977 to 2012, only 16 percent were eventually executed.

Yes: The Death Penalty Is Applied Fairly

No: The Death Penalty Is Not Applied Fairly

Chapter 4: How Should US Death Penalty Practices Be Reformed?

In cases of convicted murderers of horrible crimes and where guilt is certain, there is no good argument against the death penalty. Cherry-picking questionable death-row cases to underscore the fallibility of capital punishment, as opponents of the system typically do, does not render the death penalty unjust or unwarranted for those murderers whose guilt is beyond any doubt.

Foreword

By definition, controversies are "discussions of questions in which opposing opinions clash" (Webster's Twentieth Century Dictionary Unabridged). Few would deny that controversies are a pervasive part of the human condition and exist on virtually every level of human enterprise. Controversies transpire between individuals and among groups, within nations and between nations. Controversies supply the grist necessary for progress by providing challenges and challengers to the status quo. They also create atmospheres where strife and warfare can flourish. A world without controversies would be a peaceful world; but it also would be, by and large, static and prosaic.

The Series' Purpose

The purpose of the Current Controversies series is to explore many of the social, political, and economic controversies dominating the national and international scenes today. Titles selected for inclusion in the series are highly focused and specific. For example, from the larger category of criminal justice, Current Controversies deals with specific topics such as police brutality, gun control, white collar crime, and others. The debates in Current Controversies also are presented in a useful, timeless fashion. Articles and book excerpts included in each title are selected if they contribute valuable, long-range ideas to the overall debate. And wherever possible, current information is enhanced with historical documents and other relevant materials. Thus, while individual titles are current in focus, every effort is made to ensure that they will not become quickly outdated. Books in the Current Controversies series will remain important resources for librarians, teachers, and students for many years.

In addition to keeping the titles focused and specific, great care is taken in the editorial format of each book in the series. Book introductions and chapter prefaces are offered to provide background material for readers. Chapters are organized around several key questions that are answered with diverse opinions representing all points on the political spectrum. Materials in each chapter include opinions in which authors clearly disagree as well as alternative opinions in which authors may agree on a broader issue but disagree on the possible solutions. In this way, the content of each volume in Current Controversies mirrors the mosaic of opinions encountered in society. Readers will quickly realize that there are many viable answers to these complex issues. By questioning each author's conclusions, students and casual readers can begin to develop the critical thinking skills so important to evaluating opinionated material.

Current Controversies is also ideal for controlled research. Each anthology in the series is composed of primary sources taken from a wide gamut of informational categories including periodicals, newspapers, books, US and foreign government documents, and the publications of private and public organizations. Readers will find factual support for reports, debates, and research papers covering all areas of important issues. In addition, an annotated table of contents, an index, a book and periodical bibliography, and a list of organizations to contact are included in each book to expedite further research.

Perhaps more than ever before in history, people are confronted with diverse and contradictory information. During the Persian Gulf War, for example, the public was not only treated to minute-to-minute coverage of the war, it was also inundated with critiques of the coverage and countless analyses of the factors motivating US involvement. Being able to sort through the plethora of opinions accompanying today's major issues, and to draw one's own conclusions, can be a complicated and frustrating struggle. It is the editors' hope that Current Controversies will help readers with this struggle.

Introduction

"Although the US Supreme Court has never interpreted the Eighth Amendment's prohibition on cruel and unusual punishment to completely prevent the states from administering the death penalty, it has placed constitutional limits on the practice."

The death penalty, or capital punishment, has existed as a punishment for centuries in countries throughout the world. In the United States, the death penalty has been practiced since the founding of the country, although—as today—it has always varied by state. Since criminal sanctions are administered by the states (except in the case of federal crimes), each state determines its own policy with respect to punishment, including whether or not it allows capital punishment and, if so, for which crimes. However, the US Constitution places limits on the criminal justice practices of the states through the Eighth Amendment, which demands, "Excessive bail shall not be required, nor excessive fines imposed, nor cruel and unusual punishments inflicted." Although the US Supreme Court has never interpreted the Eighth Amendment's prohibition on cruel and unusual punishment to completely prevent the states from administering the death penalty, it has placed constitutional limits on the practice.

In 1972, the US Supreme Court, in a group of cases known collectively as *Furman v. Georgia*, determined that when the death sentence is given in a way that is arbitrary or capricious it is in violation of the Eighth Amendment. The Court reasoned that a punishment is "cruel and unusual" if the people who receive it are, as Justice Potter Stewart put it, "among a capriciously selected random handful upon whom the sentence of death has in fact been imposed." The justices expressed a variety of concerns about the way the states were administering the death penalty, including concerns that it was administered in a way that suggested racial bias. The result of the opinion was a nationwide moratorium on the death penalty while states looked at ways to avoid the unconstitutional arbitrariness identified by the Court.

Several states attempted to eliminate arbitrary discretion by juries and judges by providing sentencing guidelines for determining whether to impose the death penalty that allowed for aggravating and mitigating factors. The Supreme Court approved the revised death penalty statutes of Georgia, Florida, and Texas in 1976 in a collective case known as *Gregg v. Georgia*, noting that the death penalty itself was constitutional under the Eighth Amendment:

> Considerations of federalism, as well as respect for the ability of a legislature to evaluate, in terms of its particular State, the moral consensus concerning the death penalty and its social utility as a sanction, require us to conclude, in the absence of more convincing evidence, that the infliction of death as a punishment for murder is not without justification, and thus is not unconstitutionally severe.

The Court determined that if the sentence of death is given according to objective criteria and if the particular character of the defendant can be taken into account, the death penalty is allowed under the US Constitution.

Since the Court's decision in *Gregg*, it has placed other constitutional limits on the use of the death penalty. The Court has determined that the death penalty may not be given for the crime of rape when the victim does not die, reasoning that to do so would constitute a disproportionate punishment, in violation of the Eighth Amendment. The Court has also ruled that it is unconstitutional to give minors under the age of eighteen and the mentally handicapped a sentence of death, determining that such a punishment would be cruel and unusual and, thus, constitutionally forbidden.

Although the Supreme Court has allowed that the states have discretion in allowing capital punishment, not all states permit the death penalty. As of August 2014, thirty-two states have the death penalty and eighteen states do not. Six of the states that have banned the death penalty did so since 2007, illustrating a trend in the United States away from capital punishment. That said, a majority of Americans still support the death penalty and a majority of the states still offer death as a mode of punishment. The current debates about the death penalty in the United States are explored in *Current Controversies: Death Penalty*, illustrating the opposing viewpoints that are taken on this complicated issue.

CHAPTER 1

Is the Death Penalty Just and Ethical?

Mohawk Valley Community College Library

Overview: View of Death Penalty as Morally OK Unchanged in US

Jeffrey M. Jones

Jeffrey M. Jones is managing editor of the Gallup Poll.

The recent news about the botched execution of an Oklahoma death row inmate has not affected the way Americans view the death penalty. Sixty-one percent say the death penalty is morally acceptable, similar to the 62% who said so in 2013, although both figures are down from a high of 71% in 2006.

The results are based on Gallup's annual Values and Beliefs poll, conducted May 8–11. On April 29, an Oklahoma death row inmate given a lethal injection appeared to suffer for an extended period of time until finally dying of a heart attack. That incident led to the postponement of a second execution scheduled in Oklahoma that day and raised questions about the methods used to execute prisoners.

The case did not fundamentally alter Americans' perceptions of the death penalty, however, with a solid majority viewing it as morally acceptable. This percentage is similar to the 60% who say they favor the death penalty as punishment for murder in Gallup's October update.

But the longer-term trends reveal that Americans have become less supportive of the death penalty. Gallup first asked the moral acceptability question in 2001, with an average 66% saying it was acceptable between 2001 and the peak in 2006. Over the last three years, the percentage saying it is morally acceptable has averaged 60%.

Jeffrey M. Jones, "Overview: View of Death Penalty as Morally OK Unchanged in US," Gallup, May 15, 2014. Copyright © 2014 by The Gallup Organization. All rights reserved. Reproduced by permission.

Similarly, Americans' support for the death penalty as a punishment for murder is also trending downward. Support reached a high of 80% in 1994, but it has generally slipped since then.

Americans Still Say Lethal Injection Most Humane Form of Execution

Lethal injection has been the most common method state officials have used to execute death row inmates for many years. The American public generally approves of that approach, as the poll finds Americans overwhelmingly saying lethal injection is the most humane way to administer the death penalty. The 65% holding this view compares with between 4% and 9% who endorse another method—the electric chair, gas chamber, firing squad, or hanging—as the most humane way to execute someone sentenced to death.

Americans have long supported the death penalty, with majorities saying they favor it as a penalty for murder and believe it is morally acceptable.

Gallup has asked this question twice before, and although 23 years have elapsed since the question was last asked, the results today have changed little. In 1991, 67% said lethal injection was the most humane method for administering the death penalty, and in 1985, 56% said this.

A majority of those who view the death penalty as morally acceptable and those who view it as morally wrong say lethal injection is the most humane way to execute prisoners. However, this belief is more common among those who say the death penalty is acceptable. Notably, roughly one in four of those who say the death penalty is morally wrong volunteer that "no method" is the most humane way to execute someone.

Implications

The drawn-out death of the Oklahoma prisoner reignited the debate over whether the death penalty violates the Constitution's prohibition of "cruel and unusual" punishment. The U.S. Supreme Court invalidated state death penalty statutes in the 1972 case *Furman v. Georgia,* deciding that death sentences were often arbitrary and consequently were a form of cruel and unusual punishment. Later, in the 1976 *Gregg v. Georgia* judgment, the Supreme Court ruled that states' rewritten statutes did pass constitutional muster, leading to a resumption of the death penalty in the U.S.

Americans have long supported the death penalty, with majorities saying they favor it as a penalty for murder and believe it is morally acceptable. While both of these Gallup trends show diminished support for the death penalty in recent years, the trends were in place well before the Oklahoma case.

Q&A: Death Penalty Proponent Robert Blecker

Robert Blecker, interviewed by Rodger Jones

Robert Blecker is professor of law at New York Law School. He is interviewed by Dallas News editorial writer Rodger Jones.

Our Q&A is with New York Law School professor Robert Blecker, death penalty proponent and author. Based on thousands of hours inside maximum security prisons and on death rows in several states, his recently published crime-and-punishment memoir *The Death of Punishment* urges a fresh look at our criminal justice system.

You have heard the arguments from appellate lawyers who are trying to block executions that use untried drugs, based on the objection they might cause pain. What's your reaction?

This whole controversy obscures deeper disagreements about the death penalty itself. Abolitionists—those who oppose capital punishment—try to clog the system with specious attacks. Clearly we can administer a lethal anesthetic to painlessly kill. Why should the FDA approve the drug? This is not medicine to cure; it's poison to kill.

A massive dose of anesthetic might produce dying twitches, making it falsely appear that the condemned, completely unconscious, experiences pain. To maximize its deterrent effect, ideally punishment should *appear* painful to the public while actually experienced as painless to the punished.

I once witnessed an execution. It struck me as obscenely similar to my father-in-law's death in a hospice: The dying lay on a gurney, wrapped in white sheets, an IV in his arm, poison coursing through his veins.

Robert Blecker, interviewed by Rodger Jones, "Q&A: Death Penalty Proponent Robert Blecker," *Dallas Morning News*, April 11, 2014. Copyright © 2014. REPRINTED WITH PERMISSION OF THE DALLAS MORNING NEWS.

How we kill those we love should never resemble how we kill those we rightly detest. Thus, I too, oppose lethal injection, not because it possibly causes pain, but because it certainly causes confusion—conflating medicine with punishment.

What form of execution do you favor?

I prefer the firing squad. I would allow a representative of the victim's family, if they wanted, to take the first shot from any range, before the sharpshooters finished the execution.

In your book, you lay out the case for retributive justice, kind of a just-deserts doctrine. Please explain.

We have the responsibility to punish those who deserve it, but only to the degree they deserve it. Retributivists do not justify the death penalty by the general deterrence or safety it brings us. And we reject over-punishing no less than under-punishing. How obscene that aggravated murderers who behave well inside prison watch movies and play softball.

We must never allow our satisfaction at doing justice to deteriorate into sadistic revenge.

We also find it obscene, as the ACLU has recently documented, that 3,000 persons serve life without parole for non-violent crimes in the U.S. For all true retributivists, the past counts. Don't ask us what good will it do. Regardless of future benefits, we justify punishment because it's deserved. Let the punishment fit the crime. The past counts.

How does retribution differ from revenge, in your view?

Opponents wrongly equate retribution and revenge, because they both would inflict pain and suffering on those who have inflicted pain and suffering on us.

Whereas revenge knows no bounds, retribution must be limited, proportional and appropriately directed: The retributive punishment fits the crime. We must never allow our satisfaction at doing justice to deteriorate into sadistic revenge.

DNA tests have proven the fallibility of the U.S. justice system, something we've seen frequently in Texas. How do you defend capital punishment in light of that?

Social life proves the fallibility of every human institution. We do imperfectly define, detect, prosecute and punish crime. We have not yet provably but nevertheless have, most probably, executed an innocent person in the modern era. Any true retributivist feels sick at this thought. We support the mission of the Innocence Project.

Fortunately, as we raise the stakes we drastically reduce the mistakes. Before we sentence a defendant to life without parole, and especially before we condemn him to die, I would require a higher burden of persuasion than proof beyond a reasonable doubt. A jury should have no nagging doubts, however unreasonable. Before they sentence a person to die, a jury should be convinced beyond any residual doubt that he did it, and also be convinced "to a moral certainty" that he deserves to die.

Many times daily we risk the lives of those we love for the sake of convenience. Surely then, we will occasionally risk the lives of those we detest for the sake of justice.

You take issue with some death sentences, wondering whether the system has always targeted the "right people." Who are the "right people," and when has the system gone overboard?

We can never exactly and exhaustively define in advance the worst of the worst—those who most deserve to die. But thousands of hours documenting the lives and attitudes of convicted killers these past 25 years have shown me clear examples of who deserve to die.

As *The Death of Punishment* urges, we should reserve capital punishment for those who rape and murder, especially children or other vulnerable victims, serial killers, hired killers, torture killers, mass murderers, and terrorists.

It comes down to cruelty and viciousness, really: Did the killer exhibit intense pleasure or a selfish depraved, cold indifference? As Aristotle taught us, evil lies at the extremes.

As bizarre as this sounds, inside prisons it's nobody's job to punish.

At the same time, we should refine our death penalty statutes to eliminate other aggravating circumstances: Robbery-murder has put more killers on death row than any other aggravator, and too often unjustifiably so. Texas particularly makes a huge moral mistake, in my view, by focusing on future dangerousness, rather than past desert.

We can construct prisons to incapacitate the dangerous. We should only execute those who most deserve it. And not randomly. Refine our death penalty statutes and review the sentences of everyone on death row. Release into general population those who don't really deserve to die. The rest we should execute—worst first.

Overall, you suggest that the American system has lost its appetite for punishment. Can you explain?

As bizarre as this sounds, inside prisons it's nobody's job to punish. Consult the department of correction's mission statement in the 50 states, including Texas. You will not find the word "punishment."

Officers and prisoners in the many prisons I've visited in seven states—but not yet Texas—speak with one voice: "What a guy did out there is none of my business. I only care how he behaves once he's inside."

Vicious cowards who prey on the vulnerable, once captured, often become the best behaved—"good inmates" from corrections point of view. They live the good life inside prison, with the most privileges. Thus, even as we mouth it, we mock our basic credo of justice: Let the punishment fit the crime. Inside prison, too often, those who deserve it most, suffer least.

Explain your idea of "permanent punitive segregation" for convicted killers and how it is or isn't catching on among decision-makers.

Whether we keep or abolish death as punishment, we need to rethink prison for the worst of the worst. A jury should specially convict and condemn them to permanent punitive segregation. Life for them, every day, should be painful and unpleasant—the harshest conditions the Constitution allows.

They would eat only nutraloaf, a tasteless patty, nutritionally complete but offering no sensory pleasure. All visits should be non-contact and kept to a constitutional minimum. A person who rapes and murders a child, or tortures another to death should never touch another human being again.

These most heinous criminals would never watch TV. They would get one brief, lukewarm shower a week. Let photos of their victims adorn their cells—in their face but out of reach.

Connecticut, even as they abolished the death penalty, recently took steps in this direction. Let's reconnect crime with punishment. For the question of justice really is not whether they live or die, but how they live until they die.

Koch Death Penalty Arguments Still Persuasive

Jack Kenny

Jack Kenny writes for the New American.

The passing of former New York Mayor Ed Koch on February 1 brings to mind one of the most controversial things he ever did as a Democrat in the heart of American liberalism. In 1985, the three-term (January 1, 1978–December 31, 1989) mayor wrote an essay defending the death penalty. He even had the temerity to declare, "Life is indeed precious and I believe the death penalty helps to affirm that fact."

Though it outraged liberals and "progressives" among the nation's esteemed "intelligentsia," Koch's essay reflected the convictions of most Americans, then as now, as opinion polls have consistently shown a substantial majority in favor of the death penalty. Yet the issue has been hotly debated for decades, based on claims concerning the morality of a state-imposed sentence of death. In June 1972 the U.S. Supreme Court, in *Furman v. Georgia*, found the death penalty to be unconstitutional when sentences are handed down and executions are carried out in ways that are arbitrary or influenced by racial bias. The decision resulted in a de facto ban on executions nationwide, pending further word from the Court. They were resumed in 1976 under guidelines meant to provide greater consistency and eliminate racial discrimination in capital cases.

In broader terms, however, arguments have often centered on the issue of deterrence. Death penalty defenders have argued that the electric chair, the gas chamber, the hangman's

Jack Kenny, "Koch Death Penalty Arguments Still Persuasive," *New American*, February 18, 2013. Copyright © 2013 by New American. All rights reserved. Reproduced by permission.

noose, or lethal injection deterred people from killing others. Opponents argue the possibility of facing the death sentence has no deterrent effect on those who kill in crimes of passion or those who believe they won't get caught. One argument that defies refutation is that whomever else it may or may not deter, capital punishment surely deters the killer who has been caught, duly tried, and executed. That one will not kill again. Death penalty opponents argue, however, that we can achieve that goal just as well with sentences of life without parole.

Koch, writing at the time the electric chair was either still in use or within recent memory, cited the example of a man who boasted of being undeterred because the death penalty was not in force. "Consider the tragic death of Rosa Velez, who happened to be home when a man named Luis Vera burglarized her apartment in Brooklyn," Koch wrote. Vera admitted he shot and killed the woman. "She knew me, and I knew I wouldn't go to the chair," he later admitted.

Retribution is an essential component of justice and society, like individuals, has a right to self-defense against homicide.

Yet death penalty opponents would have us feel guilty as citizens when the state puts a killer to death for his crime or crimes. We are asked to believe that the state is hypocritical for punishing killing with killing. To recall a refrain from the 1960s, "Why do we kill people who kill people to show people that killing people is wrong?" One might say the same about a prison sentence for a kidnapper. Is the state wrong to imprison people for imprisoning people because imprisoning people is wrong? What should we do, short of treating every crime as a sickness that can be cured with shock therapy or some other form of "extreme makeover"?

Koch cited as a "curiosity of modern life" the spectacle of convicted murderers, when facing execution, lecturing the rest of society on the immorality of the death penalty. Such special pleading suggests the condemned killer is as much, if not more, sinned against than sinning. He may have killed someone in a fit of passion or desperate need for a quick financial gain. The state, on the other hand, will calmly and coolly throw the switch or inject the needle as a matter of simple retribution. An individual made a rash and foolish judgment. The state should know better.

But retribution is an essential component of justice and society, like individuals, has a right to self-defense against homicide. Again, death penalty abolitionists argue that a sentence of life without parole fulfills that need. Some death penalty defenders argue that the care and feeding of murderers until they die of old age in prison simply costs the state too much money. Opponents contend the legal costs of imposing the death penalty, after all the prisoner's appeals have been exhausted, outweighs the cost of imprisonment. Either argument is crass and hardly relevant in a debate over the sanctity of life and the demands of justice. Not everything can or should be determined by a cost-benefit analysis.

A problem with the life sentence alternative is that killers sometimes escape prison. Or they murder guards or other prisoners with impunity. Already sentenced to life, with the death penalty not available to the state, what do they have to lose? Then there is the question of proportionality. Are there not some crimes so heinous that the execution of the perpetrators is the only punishment that even remotely fits the crime?

The Bible has been argued over with more heat than light in the debate over the death penalty. "Thou shalt not kill" is undoubtedly one of the Ten Commandments, though it is clear the meaning in that context is "murder," or unlawful killing. Only committed pacifists believe killing an aggressor threatening one's own life or the life of another is inherently evil, or that killing soldiers of an invading army is murder.

And the law that came by Moses was not written for pacifists. God in the Old Testament frequently sent the Israelites off to war. And Exodus and Deuteronomy, where the Ten Commandments are found, prescribe the death penalty for a wide range of crimes. In Genesis, God is heard not only affirming the death penalty, but also offering a reason for it that anticipates Koch's argument; "Whosoever shall shed man's blood, his blood shall be shed: for man was made to the image of God" (Genesis 9:6).

If you were the parent of a six-year-old with a dozen bullet holes in his dead body, would you oppose a sentence of death for the child's killer?

Abolitionists often cite the New Testament story of the woman caught in adultery (John 8: 1–11) in an effort to enlist Jesus as a death penalty opponent. The law, the crowd pointed out, prescribed death by stoning for such an offense. (One shudders to think of the mortality rate if adultery were a capital crime in modern America.) But surely the fact that one might oppose a death sentence in some cases does not necessarily mean he would oppose it in all cases. Besides, even in those pre-Miranda times, the accused was entitled to some semblance of due process. And the gang that dragged the woman to Jesus appeared more like a lynch mob than a jury.

Koch in his essay offered the following simple and compelling argument: If we reduced the penalty for rape, he asked, would that show a greater or a lesser respect for women and human sexuality? The question really answers itself. So what does abolishing the death penalty say about our respect for life? "When we lower the penalty for murder," Koch wrote, "it signals a lessened regard for the value of the victim's life." The mayor also dismissed as "sophistic nonsense" the argument advanced by some death penalty opponents that a life sentence is actually a harsher punishment than the penalty of death. "A few killers may decide not to appeal a death sentence," he wrote, "but the overwhelming majority make every effort to stay alive."

Here is another question: Suppose the killer of the 20 first-graders and six faculty members at Sandy Hook School in Newtown, Connecticut, last December had not killed himself, but were sitting now in a jail cell awaiting trial. Suppose he were found legally sane. Would death penalty foes oppose the ultimate penalty for him? The question would be hypothetical even under those conditions, since Connecticut has abolished its death penalty. But if you were the parent of a six-year-old with a dozen bullet holes in his dead body, would you oppose a sentence of death for the child's killer?

No doubt some people would, holding fast to their allegedly humane principles. Such principles are marvelously flexible, however, as seen from the fact that many of the most ardent opponents of the death penalty are equally zealous in support of "abortion rights." They would spare the lives of convicted murderers, but not the lives of innocent pre-born babies. Their consciences forbid them from opposing a woman's "right to choose," even if it has cost an estimated 55 million lives since the U.S. Supreme Court's 1973 *Roe v. Wade* ruling prohibiting states from protecting prenatal life. Ours has been an age peculiar for the passage of laws to protect human health and the repeal of laws to defend human life. And yet we have consolation with us: At least those aborted in the womb have been spared the dangers of second-hand smoke.

What more should we expect from the purveyors of "progressive" thought in what T.S. Eliot described as "an age which advances progressively backwards?"

Why Christians Should Support the Death Penalty

R. Albert Mohler Jr.

R. Albert Mohler Jr. is president of the Southern Baptist Theological Seminary.

The death penalty has been part of human society for millennia, understood to be the ultimate punishment for the most serious crimes.

But, should Christians support the death penalty now, especially in light of the controversial execution Tuesday [April 29, 2014] in Oklahoma?

This is not an easy yes or no question.

The Bible's Teaching on the Death Penalty

On the one hand, the Bible clearly calls for capital punishment in the case of intentional murder.

In Genesis 9:6, God told Noah that the penalty for intentional murder should be death: "Whoever sheds the blood of man, by man shall his blood be shed, for God made man in his own image."

The death penalty was explicitly grounded in the fact that God made every individual human being in his own image, and thus an act of intentional murder is an assault upon human dignity and the very image of God.

In the simplest form, the Bible condemns murder and calls for the death of the murderer. The one who intentionally takes life by murder forfeits the right to his own life.

In the New Testament, the Apostle Paul instructs Christians that the government "does not bear the sword in vain."

R. Albert Mohler Jr., "Why Christians Should Support the Death Penalty," CNN, May 1, 2014. Copyright © 2014 by CNN. All rights reserved. Reproduced by permission.

Indeed, in this case the magistrate "is the servant of God, an avenger who carries out God's wrath on the evildoer" [Romans 13:4].

On the other hand, the Bible raises a very high requirement for evidence in a case of capital murder.

The act of murder must be confirmed and corroborated by the eyewitness testimony of accusers, and the society is to take every reasonable precaution to ensure that no one is punished unjustly.

While the death penalty is allowed and even mandated in some cases, the Bible also reveals that not all who are guilty of murder and complicity in murder are executed.

Just remember the biblical accounts concerning Moses, David and Saul, later known as Paul.

Christian thinking about the death penalty must begin with the fact that the Bible envisions a society in which capital punishment for murder is sometimes necessary, but should be exceedingly rare.

The Bible also affirms that the death penalty, rightly and justly applied, will have a powerful deterrent effect.

We have lost the cultural ability to declare murder—even mass murder—to be deserving of the death penalty.

In a world of violence, the death penalty is understood as a necessary firewall against the spread of further deadly violence.

Seen in this light, the problem we face today is not with the death penalty, but with society at large.

American society is quickly conforming to a secular worldview, and the clear sense of right and wrong that was Christianity's gift to Western civilization is being replaced with a much more ambiguous morality.

We have lost the cultural ability to declare murder—even mass murder—to be deserving of the death penalty.

The Problems with the Death Penalty

We have also robbed the death penalty of its deterrent power by allowing death penalty cases to languish for years in the legal system, often based on irrational and irrelevant appeals.

While most Americans claim to believe that the death penalty should be supported, there is a wide disparity in how Americans of different states and regions think about the issue.

Furthermore, Christians should be outraged at the economic and racial injustice in how the death penalty is applied. While the law itself is not prejudiced, the application of the death penalty often is.

There is very little chance that a wealthy white murderer will ever be executed. There is a far greater likelihood that a poor African-American murderer will face execution.

Why? Because the rich can afford massively expensive legal defense teams that can exhaust the ability of the prosecution to get a death penalty sentence.

This is an outrage, and no Christian can support such a disparity. As the Bible warns, the rich must not be able to buy justice on their own terms.

There is also the larger cultural context. We must recognize that our cultural loss of confidence in human dignity and the secularizing of human identity has made murder a less heinous crime in the minds of many Americans.

Most would not admit this lower moral evaluation of murder, but our legal system is evidence that this is certainly true.

Opposition to the Death Penalty

We also face a frontal assault upon the death penalty that is driven by legal activists and others determined to bring legal execution to an end in America.

Controversy over an execution this week in Oklahoma will bring even more attention to this cause, but most Americans will be completely unaware that this tragedy was caused by the inability of prison authorities to gain access to drugs for lethal injection that would have prevented those complications.

Opponents of the death penalty have, by their legal and political action, accomplished what might seem at first to be impossible—they now demand action to correct a situation that they largely created.

I believe that Christians should hope, pray and strive for a society in which the death penalty, rightly and rarely applied, would make moral sense.

Their intention is to make the death penalty so horrifying in the public mind that support for executions would disappear. They have attacked every form of execution as "cruel and unusual punishment," even though the Constitution itself authorizes the death penalty.

It is a testament to moral insanity that they have successfully diverted attention from a murderer's heinous crimes and instead put the death penalty on trial.

Christian Support for the Death Penalty

Should Christians support the death penalty today?

I believe that Christians should hope, pray and strive for a society in which the death penalty, rightly and rarely applied, would make moral sense.

This would be a society in which there is every protection for the rights of the accused, and every assurance that the social status of the murderer will not determine the sentence for the crime.

Christians should work to ensure that there can be no reasonable doubt that the accused is indeed guilty of the crime. We must pray for a society in which the motive behind capital punishment is justice, and not merely revenge.

We must work for a society that will honor every single human being at every point of development and of every race and ethnicity as made in God's image.

We must hope for a society that will support and demand the execution of justice in order to protect the very existence of that society. We must pray for a society that rightly tempers justice with mercy.

Should Christians support the death penalty today? I believe that we must, but with the considerations detailed above.

At the same time, given the secularization of our culture and the moral confusion that this has brought, this issue is not so clear-cut as some might think.

I do believe that the death penalty, though supported by the majority of Americans, may not long survive in this cultural context.

It is one thing to support the death penalty. It is another thing altogether to explain it, fix it, administer it and sustain it with justice.

We are about to find out if Americans have the determination to meet that challenge. Christians should take leadership to help our fellow citizens understand what is at stake.

God affirmed the death penalty for murder as he made his affirmation of human dignity clear to Noah. Our job is to make it clear to our neighbors.

The US Death Penalty Violates Human Rights

David A. Love

David A. Love is the executive director of Witness to Innocence, a national organization of exonerated former death row prisoners and their families.

There's a buzz about the death penalty in America these days. And nearly all of the conversation focuses not on how to maintain the practice, but rather on abolition.

The Death Penalty in the States

Connecticut just decided [2012] to repeal the death penalty, following the lead of Illinois, New Mexico and New Jersey in recent years. Meanwhile, California voters will vote on a ballot measure that would eliminate one-quarter of the nation's death row.

Faced with the high cost, lack of deterrent effect and the inevitability of executing innocent people, some states are taking another look. Moreover, given the appalling specter of prosecutors striking black jurors and other forms of racial misconduct, North Carolina and Kentucky have enacted racial justice legislation to overturn racially biased death sentences.

With the European Union enacting an export ban on lethal injection chemicals to the U.S., states are scrambling to find out how to kill people. With diminished supplies, states are faced with the option of suspending executions altogether, or like a violence addict, purchasing the poisons on the black market. In other cases such as Ohio, they have abandoned the

David A. Love, "The Death Penalty is the Tip of America's Human Rights Iceberg," *Huffington Post*, May 16, 2012. Copyright © 2012 by David A. Love. All rights reserved. Reproduced by permission.

commonly-used, three-drug protocol in favor of a single drug such as pentobarbital—a more commonly found substance used to euthanize animals.

And so, as people are still put down like dogs in the land of the free—despite the momentum for abolition—capital punishment represents America's human rights blind spot. But really, this is about more than executions. Rather, it speaks to a nation that often pays lip service to upholding human rights, but debases and denigrates human life through its actions. The result is a callous culture of violence, neglect and disregard.

One Among Many Violations

The U.S. ranked fifth in the world in capital punishment last year, in league with China, Saudi Arabia, Iran and Iraq. A world leader in executions, America is the world's foremost leader in prisons. The U.S. claims one-twentieth of the global population, but one-quarter of the world's prisoners. A majority of these prisoners are poor and of color, poorly educated, poorly represented in the courtroom and failed by the system. The warehousing of people is big business, an unseemly union of criminal justice policy and profit motive.

The death penalty is the tip of the iceberg when it comes to human rights violations in the U.S.

Is it an accident that the world's prison leader also ranks near the bottom in income inequality, boasts the largest income inequality in the developed world? Hardly not. Inequality in the land of opportunity is far more than in Europe, Canada, Australia and South Korea, but also more than nearly all of Asia, West Africa and North Africa. The top 1 percent of Americans enjoy far more than elsewhere in the West in terms of executive pay and policies favoring the rich. This, as

America's 99 percent receive far less government support for health insurance, daycare, pensions and education.

Meanwhile, as the U.S. preaches democracy to the rest of the world, it enacts voter ID laws that could potentially disenfranchise millions of citizens. Harder to vote, yet easier to purchase a gun. Leading the industrialized nations in handgun proliferation and firearms deaths, America is truly what Martin Luther King called "the greatest purveyor of violence in the world today." Lax gun laws, "shoot to kill" legislation and laws allowing concealed weapons in schools, churches, sports arenas and bars reflect the power of corporate arms manufacturers in U.S. politics. Made in America, the violence is exported to Mexico in the form of illegal weapons fueling the drug war carnage.

And this culture of violence extends to the death penalty, in a country conditioned by years of dehumanization, normalized through slavery and Jim Crow lynching. The death penalty is the tip of the iceberg when it comes to human rights violations in the U.S. It might be the most disturbing example of the human rights challenges facing the nation, and the challenges are many.

Against Capital Punishment

Charles C.W. Cooke

Charles C.W. Cooke writes for the National Review.

Let's Choose Not to Kill When We Don't Have To

Since the state of Oklahoma "botched" its execution of Clayton Lockett last week, the media have turned their fleeting attentions to the death penalty—mostly in a tone of voice that can best be described as censorious. This website, in turn, has pushed back against the impulse, Dennis Prager asking rhetorically whether "the side that can't muster outrage over murder victims" is "really the one with a heart," John Lott Jr. doing an admirable job questioning some of the sloppy thinking on the abolitionists' side, and Jonah Goldberg taking to heart Radley Balko's wise assessment that "both sides of the death-penalty debate have irreconcilable moral convictions" and concluding, for his part, that "Lockett deserved to die for what he did." "Everything else," Goldberg wrote, having run through the objections, "amounts to changing the subject, and it won't convince me otherwise."

National Review being a magazine that features a variety of different views, I thought it was about time that someone made the opposite case. So, here it is: I dissent.

While I am in agreement with their goals, I should say that many of the cases that capital punishment's opponents level against the institution strike me as being embarrassingly weak. The fashionable claim that the Eighth Amendment outlaws the practice as "cruel and unusual punishment" is not merely historically and legally illiterate—the worst of the liv-

Charles C.W. Cooke, "Against Capital Punishment: Let's Choose Not to Kill When We Don't Have To," *National Review Online*, May 8, 2014. Copyright © 2014 by National Review. All rights reserved. Reproduced by permission.

ing constitutionalists' political opportunism—but a transparent and counter-productive attempt to take away from the people a question that is ultimately theirs to decide. Also unconvincing: the breathless suggestions that a particular form of execution's causing us problems renders the whole kit and caboodle unjust (why not find a better way of carrying out the death penalty?); a popular meme that puts the United States on a similar moral plane as other users of the death penalty such as Iran, China, and North Korea—it matters, after all, for what and how you are sentencing people to death; and the insinuation that the system is inherently "racist"—which, in our era at least, appears to be highly questionable.

Better, but not perfect, is the proposition that the state's fallibility and death's finality make dangerous bedfellows. This is indisputably true. But even this line is ultimately limited in its usefulness, implying as it does that if we had perfect information, equitable sentencing, and a reliable means of offing the unwanted, then killing the guilty would be acceptable. In my view, it would not, and this, I think, is the point that should be most forcefully made. Rather than waste their time with baubles, advocates would do much better to subjugate their ancillary arguments to their essential objection: That we shouldn't be choosing to execute anybody when we don't have to.

By and large, we execute people in the United States by choice *and not by necessity.*

To my mind, this question is primarily an ethical one: Namely, "When is it acceptable to kill?" As a general rule, the best answer to this seems to be "sometimes." Mohandas Gandhi was an admirable man in many ways, but his pacifism took on a self-destructive bent that I would not recommend Americans emulate, culminating in the suggestion that the Jews of Nazi Germany should respond to the unimaginable violence that was perpetrated against them by committing mass suicide. The unfortunate truth is that, in a whole host of situations, we really do have little choice but to kill. If soldiers come over the border, guns blazing in our direction, what can we do but to fire back? When a woman is confronted by a rapist who is immune to reason and unwilling to respond to her refusals, she has little choice but to fight—to the death if needs be. If one's home is invaded and the lives of one's family members are threatened, deadly force is a wholly appropriate—and arguably mandatory—response. Life is precious. But, by its very nature, holistic pacifism has a poor answer to the question of *which* life is more precious, and when they are pitted against one another, pacifists tend to choose the lives of the aggressors while non-pacifists tend to choose the lives of the targeted.

Still, in making the case for self-defense, one needs to tease out some crucial distinctions. If a man breaks into my house and threatens me and my family, I have every right to shoot him dead. But it seems reasonable to presume that this right lasts only *for as long as he remains a threat*. What if I neutralize the threat without having to use deadly force? What if I point a gun at an attacker and he drops to the floor shouting, "Don't shoot"? What if I keep the gun trained on him and then call the police? What if I bind his hands behind his back and then involve the authorities? Would it still be acceptable for me to execute him for having put me in peril? I think not.

This situation is analogous to the death penalty in an important way. Nobody would deny that a police officer or regular citizen should be able to defend himself in the line of duty. Nevertheless, once he is safe we would all expect him to try to keep his suspect alive. Why? Well, partly because we value due process: It is, after all, not the officer's responsibility to sentence the accused to death, but his obligation to submit him to his peers for judgment. But, I'd venture, we also expect him to spare his charge because we draw a moral distinction between people who are threatening us and people who are not. Morally, does this calculation really change if the guilty person has been through a court?

The analogy is not perfect. But, by and large, we execute people in the United States by *choice* and not by necessity: as retribution, or as an example to others (which we call "deterrence"), or because it brings closure to the bereaved. We do it not so that those inside the prison gates might be safer, but so that those outside feel that justice has been served—performing in ceremony what Albert Camus called "the most premeditated of murders." Those we kill may be hideous, and their behavior may have been unspeakable. But we are appalled by them because their actions contrast so sharply with what we believe we are capable of, prompting us to share glances and to whisper in shock: "In a million years on earth, we wouldn't do anything like that."

Let's not.

CHAPTER 2

Does the Death Penalty Serve the Public Good?

Overview: The Cost of the Death Penalty

Richard Williams

Richard Williams is a policy specialist at the National Conference of State Legislatures.

The question of whether capital punishment is an acceptable way to administer justice has long perplexed the nation's lawmakers and divided its citizens.

Traditional arguments pit those who believe the death penalty has no place in a civilized society against supporters who see it as an appropriate deterrent and punishment for the most heinous crimes.

Capital punishment's unstable history demonstrates how contentious the debate has been. In 1972, the U.S. Supreme Court suspended the death penalty on the grounds it violated the Eighth Amendment's prohibition against cruel and unusual punishment. The decision voided existing statutes in 40 states. Then in 1976, the court reauthorized capital punishment, enabling states to reenact their death penalty statutes. Thirty-seven did, but three of those—Illinois, New Jersey and New Mexico—have abolished their laws since 2007. With those changes, 16 states currently do not use capital punishment.

A Costly Conviction

Although the debate continues to be rooted in philosophical arguments, the recent legislative action abolishing the death penalty has been spurred by practical concerns.

Richard Williams, "The Cost of Punishment," *State Legislatures*, vol. 37 no. 7, July–August 2011, pp. 55–56. Copyright © 2011 by The National Conference of State Legislatures. All rights reserved. Reproduced by permission.

New Jersey abolished its death penalty in 2007 in large part because the state had spent $254 million over 21 years administering it without executing a single person.

"It makes more sense fiscally to have inmates be sentenced to life imprisonment without parole than to have them sit on death row and to go through the appeals process," says Senator Christopher "Kip" Bateman, the bill's sponsor. "New Jersey is going through tough times financially and any decision that is ethical in nature and promotes fiscal responsibility is a win-win for the state."

New Mexico lawmakers followed in 2009, ending capital punishment over similar cost concerns.

Many state-initiated analyses . . . have found administering capital punishment is significantly more expensive than housing prisoners for life without parole.

"There is no more inefficient law on the books than the death penalty," says Representative Antonio "Moe" Maestas, co-sponsor of the bill to repeal it. "It sounds very callous and shallow to talk about cost, but we spend other people's money, and we have to consider scarce resources."

Maestas believes his perspective is particularly persuasive because it's rooted in pragmatism rather than personal idealism. "The bottom line is, I don't care if the most heinous criminals die. They should. But capital punishment is very expensive for our state, and we have to find the best use of taxpayer dollars and prosecutorial resources. How many other murders and violent crimes cases could be prosecuted with the resources from one death penalty case?"

A Punishment Worth Preserving

Many state-initiated analyses—including reports from Michigan, New Mexico and South Dakota—have found administering capital punishment is significantly more expensive than housing prisoners for life without parole.

A study released last month [June 2011] found California has spent more than $4 billion on capital punishment since 1978, executing 13 criminals. That's about $184 million more a year than life sentences would have cost.

Much of the cost results from litigating numerous appeals during the convict's time on death row, where the average inmate spends 13 years prior to execution.

This lengthy process also influenced Bateman's decision to sponsor an abolishment bill. "I spoke to many families who went through trying emotional times during the appeals for death row inmates," he says. "Transferring an inmate from death row to life without parole allows for the aggrieved families to have a sense of calmness in their life without having to relive the tragic events over and over again."

Many believe, however, the punishment is worth preserving even though it is expensive, if it can be made more manageable.

Illinois suspended capital punishment for 11 years before abolishing it in March 2011. When former Governor George Ryan instituted the moratorium, his intent was to give Illinois time to study and improve its capital punishment procedures.

Without the death penalty . . . there is no adequate punishment for the most vicious criminals.

During the moratorium, the Illinois Capital Punishment Commission and Reform Study Committee made several recommendations for improvement, including requiring the state Supreme Court to review all death sentences, setting minimum standards for DNA evidence, and increasing funding for indigent defense. The committee also recommended a full cost analysis, but it was never conducted.

The moratorium was not lifted and many, including Representative Jim Durkin, believe the reforms were not given an adequate chance. "This was not about frustration over a system that could not be made workable," he says. "This is strictly about abolitionists being morally opposed to the death penalty. That's fine, but be honest about it."

Without the death penalty, Durkin believes, there is no adequate punishment for the most vicious criminals. "A lot of these other arguments will not matter when someone is faced with the murder of a loved one."

One Crime Changes Minds

In Connecticut, the state's capital punishment abolishment debate took place at the same time as the trials for one of the most horrific crimes in the state's history, a home invasion that resulted in the murder of three members of the Petit family.

One of the killers, Steven Hayes, was convicted and sentenced to death earlier this year. Joshua Komisarjevsky, his accused accomplice, is set to go on trial in September. Many fear that making any change to Connecticut's current death penalty will make it unavailable to punish these men.

"If there were ever a case to merit the death penalty, this would be it," says Senator John Kissel. "And if the bill passed, while not retroactive, it could give these men grounds for appeal."

During the General Assembly's 2011 capital penalty debate, the Office of Fiscal Analysis reported Connecticut spends $3.3 million a year on death row cases and has performed only one execution since reinstating capital punishment in 1977. Lawmakers also heard from James Tillman, who spent 16 years in prison before DNA testing exonerated him. Some worry similar tests may one day prove the state has performed wrongful executions.

"A government that cannot guarantee the absolute accuracy of its proceedings should not take to itself the power of taking a human life," said Senator Martin Looney, referring to the Tillman case.

"Once someone is killed they are dead forever," says Senator Edith Prague, a long-time supporter of the death penalty. "Between the cost of capital punishment and the recent exonerations of innocent people, I have decided to generally support repeal."

But Prague ultimately changed her mind and cast the deciding vote against repeal after meeting with Dr. William Petit, the sole survivor of the Connecticut home invasion that robbed him of his family.

"If repeal comes up in the future, I will support it," she says. "The difference with this case is that these are the guys who did it. Their identity is not in doubt, and after meeting with Dr. Petit I know this is the right thing to do."

A Legislative See-Saw

With passionate proponents on each side, the death penalty will likely be on a repeal/reinstate see-saw indefinitely. This year, lawmakers in New Jersey and New Mexico have debated legislation to once again reinstate capital punishment. Although it's unlikely either bill will pass in 2011, the issue will be raised again in the future.

"There are certain heinous crimes that rise to the level of warranting the death penalty—killing a child, murdering a police officer, acts of terrorism," says Senator Robert Singer, the bill's sponsor in New Jersey. "Our old law had problems, but problems that can be fixed."

The Death Penalty Is an Effective Punishment

Derek Hunter

Derek Hunter is a Washington, DC-based writer, radio host, and political strategist who contributes frequently to the online magazine Townhall.

This week [August 18–24, 2013] has pissed me off. It's been a week filled with news I'd rather forget, but really, it's one we all should remember. It should be a rallying cry, an opportunity for those interested in justice to reform a broken system and expedite a punishment reserved for a deserving few.

A Horrific Murder

A college baseball player from Australia was murdered in Duncan, Okla., because three monsters were bored. The sheer convergence of bad parenting required to bring these three together and have none of them, not one, object to the idea of murdering a random stranger for lack of anything to do is as criminal as their murderous act. Their parents should sit in court next to them, charged as accessories.

The mother of Chancey Luna, one of the accused, told an Australian TV reporter she knew her son didn't do this because he was home at the time—she saw him. A few minutes later, she said she knew in her "heart" he couldn't have done this. If I had a child accused of something so heinous and I had an iron-clad alibi like "I was with him at the time," that's all I would be saying. That's not what she's saying. She's saying he's too respectful to have done something like this. But he, like every child, "likes to fight." Sick.

Derek Hunter, "The Ultimate Punishment," *Townhall*, August 25, 2013. Copyright © 2013 by Derek Hunter. All rights reserved. Reproduced by permission.

Chancey wasn't born evil. He became that way either through horrible parenting or horribly neglectful parenting. Whatever the case, this woman and her counterparts who created the other two evil bipeds should sit in prison with their progeny, released only after they're put to a justifiable death. Let the parents live the rest of their miserable lives with the pain their creatures imposed on the family of Christopher Lane.

A Brutal Attack

Then we move to Spokane, Wash.

Waiting for justice to happen in death penalty cases has become an inexcusably long process for families of victims.

Delbert Belton is a hero. Well, Delbert Belton was a hero. On Wednesday night, Belton, an 88-year-old veteran of World War II, became a victim of two teenage sub-human animals who beat him to death for reasons unknown. Belton, wounded in the Battle of Okinawa, was heading to a regular pool game he played weekly with his caregiver when these wastes of human flesh attacked him. He died the next day.

As of this writing, one of these beings has been arrested, the other remains at large (hopefully to be slowly run over by a steamroller or eaten alive by small woodland creatures rather than be taken into custody). May they both be slowly fed into wood chippers one appendage at a time starting with the one between their legs.

As for why these disgusting displays of inhumanity happened, I don't care. I don't want to understand these monsters, I want to eliminate them. May they be removed from the gene pool before they have a chance to infect it with their DNA.

The Impact of Opposition

Oklahoma and Washington have the death penalty, but they aren't Texas. Waiting for justice to happen in death penalty cases has become an inexcusably long process for families of victims. From 1984 to 2006, the average number of months spent on death row has increased from 74 to 145. Waiting more than 12 years for justice to be done is, in many cases, longer than the lives of the victims these killers took to get there in the first place.

In 1981, progressive hero Mumia Abu-Jamal murdered Philadelphia police officer Daniel Faulkner during a traffic stop of Mumia's brother. He shot Officer Faulkner point-blank in the face. He was sentenced to death for this disgusting murder in 1982, but anti-justice crusaders and liberal politicians and celebrities managed to deny the Faulkner family the justice they deserved and the law demanded. In 2011, Abu-Jamal's death sentence was commuted to life in prison without the possibility of parole. He'd spent 30 years on death row when he only allowed Daniel Faulkner to live 26. Only to the most disgusting corners of the progressive mind can this be seen as "justice."

But that is what progressives call it—justice. Collecting money from co-workers, friends and family members of a murder victim to provide housing, food, cable, Internet and education to the person who took a loved one from their lives—to them, that is justice.

The death penalty needs reforming. Just as the introduction of DNA evidence has freed many innocent people from death row, it also should have decreased the wait time for execution. That would be justice. But the goal of the anti-justice progressive movement is the abolition of the death penalty, not its effective use.

An Equalizer for Justice

Whether you believe in an afterlife or not, the death penalty is the greatest equalizer for justice for society's greatest monsters.

If you believe this world is all there is, that when you die you're done, then a bad day in prison is better than not existing at all. If you believe in Hell, the worst day in prison is better than the best day in Hell.

Some people knowingly do things that forfeit their right to experience even the bad things in life. And given the existence of prison weddings and conjugal visits, the sooner we weed these creatures from the herd the better. Progressives will tell you the death penalty doesn't deter crime, and that's true. It's also irrelevant. Some people are so evil and/or stupid that they don't care that they'll be executed for their actions. But where the death penalty works, where it has a 100 percent success rate, is recidivism. No executed criminal has ever harmed another innocent human being.

We had two examples of sub-human activity that is deserving of the ultimate penalty—five people whose actions should be met with the absolute justice we can bestow. They probably won't get it. A deal will be cut, or even if they do they'll live long, unproductive lives on the public dole.

The Death Penalty Protects Society from the Most Evil Criminals

Matt K. Lewis

Matt K. Lewis is a contributing editor at TheWeek.com and a senior contributor for The Daily Caller.

On Tuesday night [April 29, 2014], Oklahoma prisoner Clayton Lockett died of a heart attack after the lethal injection cocktail that was supposed to kill him didn't work.

A Botched Execution

Pretty much everyone admits that the execution of this convicted murderer was "botched." My colleague Andrew Cohen bemoans the apparent judicial failings that led up to the failed execution. The White House declared that the whole thing fell short of "humane standards."

This is regrettable. But I won't be losing any sleep over it.

Now obviously, a speedy and painless execution would have been better than what Lockett endured. But when you shoot a 19-year-old woman, and then watch as your buddies bury her alive, you sort of forfeit the right to complain about such things.

Of course, my writing this will make me a pariah to the liberal people arguing that this monster should be treated more compassionately.

In any event, this failed execution in Oklahoma has catapulted the topic of capital punishment back into the national spotlight. So this is perhaps a good opportunity to explain

Matt K. Lewis, "The Conservative Case for Capital Punishment," *The Week*, May 1, 2014. Copyright © 2014 by The Week. All rights reserved. Reproduced by permission.

why a "bleeding heart conservative" such as yours truly still supports the death penalty (if only in cases of especially heinous acts.)

Political Leanings and the Death Penalty

This isn't a clear-cut Right versus Left issue, of course. A lot of conservatives oppose capital punishment. Some social conservatives see support of the death penalty as inconsistent with opposition to abortion. (The difference, of course, is that unborn babies are innocent.)

To many liberals, it seems that it is deemed more civilized—more evolved—to care about the life of a murderer (or the Nevada desert tortoise) than that of an unborn child (or, for that matter, Lockett's 19-year-old victim). I will never understand this way of thinking, but the very words we use imply we believe it. As Erick Erickson has said, "For liberals a botched execution is when the convict dies, a botched abortion is when the innocent live."

I believe in second chances. I believe in reform and rehabilitation. But I also believe in evil.

Other small-government conservatives and libertarians argue that it is inconsistent for people who already distrust big government to grant it the power of life and death over its citizens. As a conservative who believes in *ordered* liberty, and that it is a responsibility of government to protect its citizens, this argument doesn't dissuade me—especially now that DNA testing can and should be used to exonerate the wrongly accused.

Declining crime rates have also given a new crop of conservative reformers the luxury of re-evaluating the "tough on crime" policies that were birthed out of necessity amid the crime and lawlessness of the 1970s, when it seemed the center could not hold. This was around the time when Irving Kristol described a neoconservative as "a liberal mugged by reality." My guess is that the declining crime rate helps explain why a "shrinking majority of Americans" favor the death penalty today. This seems to be a new trend. The death penalty was once so popular—and the "soft on crime" tag so damaging— that presidential candidate Bill Clinton refused to grant clemency to a mentally impaired man named Rickey Ray Rector. This case is reminiscent of the Lockett incident, in that, as the *AP* reported, "The execution was delayed by nearly an hour because medical personnel were not able to find a suitable vein in which to inject the solution."

Now, count me among those who believe mandatory minimum sentences for minor drug crimes ought to be reconsidered—and who think it's a mistake to take somebody who is guilty of possession of a small amount of marijuana and put them in a cage with violent criminals. (Pat Nolan of Prison Fellowship probably put it best when he said. "We have prisons for people we're afraid of, but we've been filling them with folks we're just mad at.")

I believe in second chances. I believe in reform and rehabilitation. But I also believe in evil.

While capital punishment may not be a deterrent (the infrequency of its use almost guarantees this), the recidivism rate is astonishingly low.

The Proper Use of the Death Penalty

Twisted rapists and murderers are not in the same universe of criminal as drug users and thieves. So even as we slash mandatory minimum sentences and reform our prison system, I do not believe we should abandon capital punishment for most extreme cases.

You really can't take someone like Clayton Lockett and reform him—or, at least, the odds of doing so are unfathomable. This wasn't a crime of passion. He didn't walk into his house, see his wife in bed with another man, fly into a rage, kill him, and then immediately feel remorse. He shot a 19-year-old woman and then watched his friends bury her alive. Try to reform that.

So what can you do? You *certainly* can't put him back on the street. You could give him life in prison and a PlayStation 3. But as the son of a prison guard from Maryland, let me assure you: Inmates who have no hope of earning an early release also have no incentive not to harm or kill correctional officers or other inmates. And solitary confinement is arguably a crueler and more unusual form of punishment than the death penalty.

And there's also this: While capital punishment may not be a deterrent (the infrequency of its use almost guarantees this), the recidivism rate is astonishingly low. I mean, there are very few repeat offenders.

So yes, we ought to make sure we get to the bottom of what went wrong with this lethal injection. But no, we shouldn't do too much hand-wringing and pearl-clutching along the way. At the end of the day, the death penalty should be safe, legal, rare—and utterly efficient.

The Death Penalty Is a Deterrent to Murder

William Tucker

William Tucker is a journalist and author of Vigilante: The Backlash Against Crime in America.

There's a concept in economics I think ought to be introduced into the public discourse. It's called the "marginal value of wealth." It means that the wealthier you become, the less each additional dollar means to you. That's why we have environmentalism—because some people have grown so affluent that they really aren't much interested in further economic development.

The Purpose of the Death Penalty

The same concept also applies to crime. There's a "marginal value of safety" that people take into account when evaluating policies such as the death penalty. Most affluent Americans now feel safe enough in their suburban retreats or gated communities with private police patrols so that they can express more concern for a condemned criminal suffering a few minutes of pain in a botched execution than for what the person did to end up on death row in the first place. (As many have pointed out, all this blundering could be fast eliminated by returning to the firing squad.)

It's a different story, however, if you're running a bodega in a low-income neighborhood or working in a 7-Eleven on a lonely Texas highway. You are completely vulnerable. You may be protected by security cameras or a locked cash register, but to an amateur with a handgun this means little. Murder is the

William Tucker, "Can We Abide the Death Penalty Any Longer?," *American Spectator*, July–August 2014. Copyright © 2014 by American Spectator. All rights reserved. Reproduced by permission.

third cause of occupational death among men, behind vehicle accidents and falls by construction workers, and the leading cause of occupational death among women. There's a very simple reason. For a criminal pulling off a holdup—or a rapist, or a "surprised" burglar caught by a homeowner—there's a very simple logic at work. The victims of your crimes are also the principal witnesses. They will call the police the minute you depart. They can identify you. They will probably testify at your trial. There's a very simple way to prevent all this: kill them.

After the death penalty was abolished, murder rates nearly tripled, rising to an all-time high in the 1980s.

The purpose of the death penalty is to draw a bright line between a felony and felony murder. If the penalty for rape or robbery is jail time, and for murder is more jail time after that, there isn't a huge incentive to prevent you from pulling the trigger. This was well known to reformers of the eighteenth century, who tried to resolve the same dilemma by eliminating the death penalty for crimes less than homicide. In *The Spirit of the Laws* (1750), Montesquieu wrote:

> It is a great abuse among us to condemn to the same punishment a person what only robs on the highway and another who robs and murders. Surely, for the public security, some difference should be made in the punishment.

> In China, those who add murder to robbery are cut in pieces: but not so the others; to this difference it is owing that though they rob in that country they never murder.

> In Russia, where the punishment of robbery and murder is the same, they always murder. The dead, they say, tell no tales.

The Deterrent Effect

In the 1960s we stopped executing people altogether. At the time homicides were at an historical low and 90 percent were "acquaintance" murders resulting from disputes between friends or relatives. "Stranger murders," which are generally committed in the course of other crimes, had been reduced to 10 percent. What happened next is well-established. After the death penalty was abolished, murder rates nearly tripled, rising to an all-time high in the 1980s. Only when the death penalty was reinstated and states started executing people in significant numbers in the 1990s did they again fall to 1960s levels. The 500,000 murders committed during this interim took more lives than any conflict in American history save the Civil War. Moreover, by the 1980s murder in the act of another crime had risen to about half the much larger total.

But of course these murders were not evenly distributed across society. Instead they are still highly concentrated in minority neighborhoods. Although African Americans make up only 13 percent of the population, they constitute 48 percent of all murder victims—93 percent of whom are killed by other blacks—and they commit 51 percent of the murders in which the case is solved. A standard argument against the death penalty is that it is racist because 40 percent of those on death row are African American. But in fact judges and juries are six times less likely to impose capital punishment if the victim is black. There is racism in the system, but it is not the kind people think.

The late Ernest van den Haag used to suggest that we should only execute people for murders on odd numbered days, just to see whether criminals would shift their activities. In fact, we have been conducting just such an experiment by race for decades. What better proof could we have that the death penalty makes a difference?

The Death Penalty Is a Flawed Form of Punishment

Brad Bushman

Brad Bushman is a professor of communication and psychology at Ohio State University.

In Old Testament times, the death penalty was used as the punishment for murder. But death was also the punishment for a number of other offenses, such as eating leavened bread during the Feast of Unleavened Bread, being a stubborn child, picking up sticks on the Sabbath day, insulting your parents, going to the Tabernacle if you are not a priest, and ignoring the verdict of a judge or priest. Today the death penalty is still used in 32 states in America, including the state I live in—Ohio.

Seven Problems with the Death Penalty

In 2007 the American Bar Association released the results of a three-year study of the death penalty. Although the American Bar Association takes no position for or against the death penalty, they issued a moratorium on the death penalty because "the process is deeply flawed." As a researcher of aggression and violence for over 25 years, I also believe the death penalty is "deeply flawed." There are at least seven serious problems with the death penalty.

The Death Penalty Models the Behavior it Seeks to Prevent

The death penalty is used to deter killers, but it models the very behavior it seeks to prevent. It teaches the lesson that it is acceptable to kill, as long as the state is the one doing the killing. Hence the term "capital punishment." This is somewhat paradoxical. As my friend Jed said, "We don't like people

Brad Bushman, "It's Time to Kill the Death Penalty," *Psychology Today*, January 19, 2014. Copyright © 2014 by Brad J. Bushman. All rights reserved. Reproduced by permission.

who kill other people, so to show everyone how much we don't like people who kill people, we are going to kill people who kill other people. It seems like capital punishment pretty much goes against everything it claims to be for." The death penalty answers violence with counter-violence. As American novelist Wendell Berry said, "Violence breeds violence. Acts of violence committed in 'justice' or in affirmation of 'rights' or in defense of 'peace' do not end violence. They prepare and justify its continuation."

The available evidence indicates that the death penalty does not reduce murder rates.

You Might Kill the Wrong Person!

William Blackstone, the English jurist, judge, and Tory politician of the 18th century, said, "Better that ten guilty persons escape than that one innocent suffer." The death penalty is irreversible, so it is critical that it be used on the actual killer. Over 140 people have been exonerated and freed from death row, such as on the basis of DNA evidence. Since the U.S. Supreme Court reinstated the death penalty in 1976, 1,362 individuals have been executed in the U.S. (as of January 16, 2014). It is difficult to know for sure how many innocent people have been executed, but it appears at least 10 have. For example, Carlos DeLuna was executed in 1989 for the 1983 murder of Wanda Lopez in Corpus Christi, Texas. The only eyewitness to the crime identified DeLuna while he was sitting in the back of a police car parked in a dimly lit lot in front of the crime scene. There was no blood, DNA evidence, or fingerprints linking DeLuna to the crime. The actual murderer was a man named Carlos Hernandez, a violent criminal who [was] very similar in appearance [to] DeLuna. Hernandez even bragged about how he had murdered Lopez and gotten someone else to take the fall for him. Family members and friends of Hernandez also confessed that he had killed Lopez. In my view, the execution of even one innocent person is too many.

The Death Penalty Does Not Deter Crime

The available evidence indicates that the death penalty does not reduce murder rates. FBI Unified Crime reports show that states with the death penalty have homicide rates 48–101% *higher* than states without the death penalty. Similarly, an international study of criminal violence analyzed data from 110 nations over a period of 74 years and found that the death penalty does not deter criminals. One reason why the death penalty might not deter criminals is that most murders are committed in a fit of rage, after an intense argument, when people rarely consider the consequences of their actions. Former U.S. Attorney General Janet Reno said: "I have inquired for most of my adult life about studies that might show that the death penalty is a deterrent. And I have not seen any research that would substantiate that point."

The U.S. is one of the few countries in the world that has executed minors under 18-years-old.

The Death Penalty Targets the Poor

Of the 22,000 murders that occur each year in the U.S., about 1% result in death sentences. Which 1% depends largely on the effectiveness of the attorney, which often depends on how much money the accused has. U.S. Supreme Court Justice Ruth Bader Ginsburg said, "People who are well represented at trial do not get the death penalty." Ginsburg also criticized the "meager" amount of money spent to defend poor people. OJ Simpson's lawyer—who received $5 million for defending him—said, "In the U.S., you're better off, if you're in the system being guilty and rich than being innocent and poor." There are no billionaires or millionaires on death row.

The Death Penalty Targets People of Color

The American Bar Association three-year study concluded: "Every state studied appears to have significant racial disparities in imposing the death penalty, particularly associated with the race of the victim, but little has been done to rectify the problem." Other statistical evidence is consistent with this conclusion. Blacks make up 12% of the U.S. population, but they make up 48% of those on death row (55% of those on death row are people of color). The odds of receiving the death penalty increase by 38% when the accused is Black. Although 50% of murders involve white victims, 80% of death penalty cases involve white victims.

The Death Penalty May Constitute "Cruel and Unusual Punishment"

The Eighth Amendment to the U.S. Constitution states: "Excessive bail shall not be required, nor excessive fines imposed, nor cruel and unusual punishments inflicted." According to the U.S. Supreme Court, punishment is cruel and unusual if it is too severe for the crime, arbitrary, is rejected throughout society, and is not more effective than a less severe penalty. The U.S. is one of the few countries in the world that has executed minors under 18-years-old. In 2005, the U.S. Supreme Court ruled that the death penalty for minors offended "evolving standards of decency" and therefore constituted "cruel and unusual punishment."

According to the American Civil Liberties Union (ACLU), "The capital punishment system is discriminatory and arbitrary and inherently violates the Constitutional ban against cruel and unusual punishment. The ACLU opposes the death penalty in all circumstances, and looks forward to the day when the United States joins the majority of nations in abolishing it." There are five methods currently used to execute people—lethal injection, electrocution, gas chamber, firing squad, and hanging—and the ACLU argues that there are significant problems with each. Consider just a few examples of several botched cases.

A prisoner generally dies within seven minutes of receiving a lethal injection. Drugs for lethal injections in the United States were obtained from Europe, where the death penalty is illegal. However legal pressures and concerns from manufacturers in Europe have made traditional execution drugs unavailable. Thus, states have been trying experimental drug cocktails for lethal injections. In a 2014 Ohio case, Dennis McGuire received a lethal injection of two new drugs (midazolam + hydromorphone). The drugs took 26 minutes to kill McGuire, as he physically struggled, choked, and gasped for air. Also in 2014, a botched execution occurred in Oklahoma with an unknown mixture of "experimental" lethal drugs. The prisoner, Clayton D. Lockett, immediately began struggling after the injection was given, and ended up dying of a massive heart attack an hour later. His attorney said: "After weeks of Oklahoma refusing to disclose basic information about the drugs for tonight's lethal injection procedures, tonight, Clayton Lockett was tortured to death." In a 2006 Florida case, Angel Nieves Diaz died 34 minutes after receiving a lethal injection. The needle apparently went through his vein and into soft tissue deep in his arm. Eyewitness reports indicate that Diaz was still moving and attempting to speak (or, perhaps, scream) more than 20 minutes into the execution. In a 2006 Ohio case, it took over 90 minutes to kill Joseph Lewis Clark. Clark could be heard moaning and groaning from behind the curtain. In a 2007 Ohio case, it took over two hours and 10 attempts to kill Christopher Newtown. It took so long that Newton was given a bathroom break. In both the Clark and Newton cases, officials had difficulty finding a vein.

In 1999 Allen Lee Davis was electrocuted in Florida. "Before he was pronounced dead . . . the blood from his mouth had poured onto the collar of his white shirt, and the blood on his chest had spread to about the size of a dinner plate, even oozing through the buckle holes on the leather chest strap holding him to the chair." Florida Supreme Court Justice Leander Shaw said that Davis "was brutally tortured to death by the citizens of Florida."

Some people may be surprised to learn that the death penalty is far more expensive to implement than life in prison without the possibility of parole.

In 1983, the electrocution of John Evans in Alabama was described in a sworn testimony by his attorney: "At 8:30 p.m. the first jolt of 1900 volts of electricity passed through Mr. Evans' body. It lasted thirty seconds. Sparks and flames erupted . . . from the electrode tied to Mr. Evans' left leg. His body slammed against the straps holding him in the electric chair and his fist clenched permanently. The electrode apparently burst from the strap holding it in place. A large puff of grayish smoke and sparks poured out from under the hood that covered Mr. Evans' face. An overpowering stench of burnt flesh and clothing began pervading the witness room. Two doctors examined Mr. Evans and declared that he was not dead." "The electrode on the left leg was re-fastened. . . . Mr. Evans was administered a second . . . jolt of electricity. The stench of burning flesh was nauseating. More smoke emanated from his leg and head. Again, the doctors examined Mr. Evans. [They] reported that his heart was still beating, and that he was still alive. At that time, I asked the prison commissioner, who was communicating on an open telephone line to Governor George Wallace, to grant clemency on the grounds that Mr. Evans was being subjected to cruel and unusual punishment. The request . . . was denied." "At 8:40 p.m., a third charge of electricity . . . was passed through Mr. Evans' body. At 8:44, the doctors pronounced him dead. The execution of John Evans took fourteen minutes." Afterwards, officials were embarrassed by what one observer called the "Barbaric ritual." The prison spokesman remarked, "This was supposed to be a very clean manner of administering death."

In 1989, Alabama executed Horace Dunkins, who had been convicted of raping and killing Lynn M. McCurry, a 26-year-old mother of four. It took two jolts of electricity, nine minutes apart, to complete the execution. After the first jolt failed to kill the prisoner (who was mildly retarded), the captain of the prison guard opened the door to the witness room and stated "I believe we've got the jacks on wrong."

Life in prison without the possibility of parole keeps the public safe from killers, while eliminating the risk of an irreversible mistake.

The Death Penalty Costs More Than Life in Prison

Some people may be surprised to learn that the death penalty is far more expensive to implement than life in prison without the possibility of parole. Take the state of California, for example. The California death penalty system costs taxpayers more than $114 million a year beyond the cost of simply keeping the convicts locked up for life. In addition, California spends $250 million per execution. In addition to state costs, there are also federal costs. The federal court system spends approximately $12 million each year on defending death row inmates in federal court. Many death penalty cases involve a long, drawn out, complex, and expensive judicial process.

The Need to Abolish the Death Penalty

The family of a 14-year-old African American George Stinney Jr.—who was executed in 1944 for allegedly killing two white girls—has asked for a retrial in light of new evidence. Stinney's trail lasted only 3 hours, and the all-white jury issued a death sentence after only 10 minutes of deliberation. This case illustrates some of the major problems with the death penalty (e.g., it is irreversible, it targets poor people, it targets people of color).

Five countries in the world account for 80% of state killings: (1) China, (2) Iran, (3) Iraq, (4) Saudi Arabia, and (5) the United States. The other five countries in the top 10 are: (6) Pakistan, (7) Yemen, (8) North Korea, (9) Vietnam, and (10) Libya. The U.S. State Department recognizes 194 independent countries around the world, and the death penalty is banned in 140 of these (72%) as of May 2103, including Russia. As an aggression and violence researcher for over 25 years, I think it is time for the U.S. to join the other 140 countries that have banned capital punishment. Murder is a terrible crime that is never justified and should always be punished. However, I believe that the punishment should be life in prison without the possibility of parole, rather than the death penalty. Life in prison without the possibility of parole keeps the public safe from killers, while eliminating the risk of an irreversible mistake.

Why Conservatives Should Oppose the Death Penalty

Radley Balko

Radley Balko blogs about criminal justice, the drug war, and civil liberties for The Washington Post.

Though I don't always agree with him, I generally find Matt Lewis to be a thoughtful conservative commentator. His response to this week's botched Oklahoma execution, "The conservative case for capital punishment," is a good example. That is, it's a thoughtful piece of writing. And I don't agree with it.

The Death Penalty in the United States

But first, a few points where I think Lewis is correct. First, whatever your position on the death penalty—and I'm an abolitionist—these botched executions aren't a particularly compelling argument against capital punishment. As Liliana Segura has written here at The Watch, the background to the current debate over what drug cocktail states use for lethal injection is complicated and convoluted. We *could* quite easily execute people with methods that are quicker, painless and more humane. There are many reasons we don't. One is that the current drug cocktail has already been approved by the U.S. Supreme Court. Switching to something else would subject a state to years of court challenges and litigation (although that is what's happening now, and it will almost certainly intensify after this week).

Another reason is appearances. If your goal is to carry out a humane execution from the perspective of the condemned,

Radley Balko, "Why Conservatives Should Oppose the Death Penalty," *Washington Post*, May 1, 2014. Copyright © 2014 by The Washington Post. All rights reserved. Reproduced by permission.

the guillotine and the firing squad are far better than lethal injection. Because of the paralytic agent used in the lethal injection cocktail, we don't really know whether the people executed this way feel pain. And this obviously isn't something that can easily be tested. But the *humanity* component has never been about the humanity of the condemned. What we actually mean by *humanity* is that we want executions to be humane from *our* perspective. We don't want to feel icky about it all. A guillotine or firing squad conjures up uncomfortable images. Lethal injection, on the other hand, is a medical procedure. So long as the paralytic agent works, there's no twitching or convulsing and there's no blood. There's little evidence anyone has died. It's the method of execution that least resembles an execution.

The argument that the people who commit particularly horrendous crimes have simply given up their right to live is a compelling one, particularly when allowing them to live means they do so at taxpayer expense.

It's also worth mentioning that, as Segura pointed out, one reason states are turning to secret drugs obtained from secret and black-market sources is that anti-death penalty activists have been successful at persuading the manufacturers of the previously used drugs to refuse to sell them for use in executions.

Lewis is also correct when he points out that the declining percentage of Americans who support the death penalty (though it's still a majority) may in part be a luxury that's come with our dramatic 20-year drop in violent crime. We should reform the police and courts for high-minded principles like equality under the law, civil liberties and fair justice, but there's no question that it's much easier to rally support for reform when the country is less fearful of crime. (It also makes it much easier to bring politicians on board.)

Finally, while I don't agree with him, I do think Lewis' argument for retributive justice—that the most heinous of killers deserve nothing short of death—is the strongest argument in favor of the death penalty. There's very little evidence that capital punishment deters violent crime. The number of convicted murderers who escape prisons is also minuscule. But the argument that the people who commit particularly horrendous crimes have simply given up their right to live is a compelling one, particularly when allowing them to live means they do so at taxpayer expense. Death penalty proponent Robert Blecker often makes this argument. (Blecker is also consistent. He argues that the death penalty *should* be painful, and it should *look* painful.) It's a moral argument, and the only real response is another moral argument. Conflicting moral arguments can't be resolved with logic or data or other empirical evidence.

Government Control of the Death Penalty

But here is where I think Lewis' piece goes wrong:

> Other small-government conservatives and libertarians argue that it is inconsistent for people who already distrust big government to grant it the power of life and death over its citizens. As a conservative who believes in *ordered* liberty, and that it is a responsibility of government to protect its citizens, this argument doesn't dissuade me—especially now that DNA testing can and should be used to exonerate the wrongly accused.

This is the most glaring contradiction in conservative support for the death penalty, and Lewis really short-shrifts it. I agree with Lewis that protecting us from criminals is a legitimate function—and, indeed, is a primary responsibility of—government. But that crime-fighting is a legitimate state function doesn't mean that it isn't susceptible to the same problems Lewis points out when criticizing the things governments do that he believes *aren't* legitimate. When it comes to the trappings of public choice and political economy, the corruption of power and tunnel-visioned public officials, the criminal justice system is no different than, say, the Environmental Protection Agency, the Department of Education or the Occupational Safety and Health Administration. Actually, there *is* one important difference: The consequences of government error in the criminal justice system are far more profound.

Police, prosecutors and crime lab technicians are just as capable at conniving, malevolence and corruption as any other human being.

Lewis is correct about DNA testing: When it's dispositive of guilt, it can now be used to both exonerate the wrongly accused and to exclude suspects who otherwise would have been wrongly accused a generation ago. But DNA is only dispositive of guilt in a small percentage of criminal cases. It can be determinative in cases in which it's clear that the killer also raped his victim. It can also be important in cases where there was a clear physical struggle between the victim and the assailant. But DNA isn't a factor in most other homicide cases. And even when it's relevant, it rarely makes or breaks a case. Killers don't always leave behind DNA. A stray hair found at the crime scene that doesn't belong to the victim could have come from the real killer. Or it could just be a stray hair that wound up at the crime scene for innocuous reasons. And in cases in which the question isn't *who* committed the homicide, but *if* a homicide was committed (that is, whether a death was accidental or intentional), DNA will rarely be relevant.

DNA testing *has* shown us that within that small percentage of cases for which it does definitively establish guilt or innocence, there's an alarmingly high rate of error. DNA testing has shown, for example, that methods of forensic analysis and types of evidence that we once thought foolproof or relatively

71

certain are far from either. DNA testing has exonerated people who were convicted because of bite-mark matching, hair and fiber matching, blood-type matching, testimony from jailhouse informants, eyewitness testimony and even fingerprint matching. (This list isn't comprehensive, of course.) Here's the thing: If the state's misuse of this sort of evidence is capable of convicting innocent people in the small percentage of criminal cases for which DNA testing is dispositive of guilt, it's almost certainly causing wrongful convictions in all of those other cases for which DNA testing is less important or irrelevant. In other words, DNA testing isn't a panacea. It's a wake-up call.

Find the exonorees who served decades in prison before they were cleared and released. Now ask them if they'd rather have been executed.

The Problem of Error

Lewis makes clear that he only supports the death penalty for the most heinous of crimes, and only for those crimes for which the defendant's guilt is certain. At first blush, it's hard to quarrel with that position. The rub is that we'll always need to draw that line somewhere. *How* heinous must the crime be? And *how* certain of guilt must we be? There have been more than a few exonerations in cases in which it seemed unimaginable that the accused people could possibly have been innocent. And yet they were. We now know that prosecutors and police are capable of fabricating and planting evidence. Not that it's necessarily common, but it happens. That means that even DNA cases aren't necessarily iron-clad. The science behind the testing may be certain, but the gathering and testing of evidence will always be done by humans and be subject to all the biases, imperfections and temptations to corruption that come with them. Or to put it in terms with which conservatives might better relate: Police, prosecutors and crime lab technicians are just as capable at conniving, malevolence and corruption as any other human being. There's nothing transformative about a government paycheck that ensures altruism, honesty or goodness; the same goes with giving someone a badge or asking him or her to swear an oath.

This was the point of my poll question here earlier this week. If you support the death penalty, you have to recognize that it will be administered by human beings, who are flawed, and then you have to acknowledge the possibility that no system of justice can be perfect. This means that over time, the probability of executing an innocent person eventually reaches 1. The question, then, isn't whether you believe an innocent person has ever been executed. The question is how many innocent people you're comfortable executing.

Finally, Lewis doesn't explicitly make this argument, but I've seen versions of it made by others on the right: *There will always be errors. So there will always be injustice. We don't scrap the whole idea of punishment because some innocents may be wrongly convicted. So why do away with a specific form of punishment?*

The answer is that death is irreversible. It's an obvious answer, but it's an important one. With a life sentence, there's always the chance to catch the mistake and ameliorate it. (It can never be fully corrected, of course.) Death penalty supporters make the argument that for an innocent person, life in prison is a punishment that's worse than death. There's a pretty easy way to test that theory. Find the exonorees who served decades in prison before they were cleared and released. Now ask them if they'd rather have been executed. I've asked a few this question. The response was some version of *Are you nuts?* I'd be surprised if you could find a single exonoree who would answer *yes*. I'd be astonished if you could find more than a couple.

Criminal Justice System Reform

One more point. I have no doubt that Lewis is sincere when he says his support for capital punishment is contingent on cleaning up the criminal justice system, fixing the mistakes we've discovered and ensuring that only the most vicious killers are executed, and in only the cases where guilt is an absolute certainty. If Lewis is up for prodding his ideological fellow travelers to support policies such as requiring a heightened burden of proof in capital cases, or restricting death penalty cases to a very narrow class of exceptionally horrific crimes (as a task force in Ohio recently recommended after a series of exonerations), that at least would be a good start.

The problem is that the politicians he and other conservatives support—the (mostly) Republican officials and legislators in states like Tennessee, Missouri, California, Florida and Arizona, among others—are *expanding* the number of crimes for which prosecutors can seek the death penalty and looking to *speed* up the rate at which they execute people. (In Ohio, prosecutors and conservative politicians have rejected the task force's recommendations.) They're doing this even as we're still discovering wrongful convictions in those states and before they've bothered to pass meaningful reforms to address the problems that led to those convictions. In fact, in many cases, they're *rejecting* reform at the same time that they're trying to churn out more executions. Even low-cost, common-sense reforms such as recording police interrogations or ensuring double-blind eyewitness lineups are tough to get by Republican politicians. (Democrats aren't much better, but that's a separate discussion.) In other words, Lewis's position is defensible in the abstract. But that isn't the way things are playing out on the ground.

People who subscribe to different belief systems sometimes have irreconcilable views on public policy issues with a strong moral component. The death penalty is one of those issues. But conservatives are supposed to be skeptical of government. That *is* a fundamental part of their belief system. And, except perhaps war, there's no issue for which the consequences of government error or abuse of power are more absolute, irreversible and profound. Even if they support the idea of capital punishment in principle, it ought to be one of the *last* issues for which conservatives would be willing to abandon that skepticism. Yet it seems to be one of the issues for which their skepticism is most negotiable.

The Death Penalty Is Too Costly for Society

Richard C. Dieter

Richard C. Dieter is executive director of the Death Penalty Information Center.

One of the most common misperceptions about the death penalty is the notion that the death penalty saves money because executed defendants no longer have to be cared for at the state's expense. If the costs of the death penalty were to be measured at the time of an execution, that might indeed be true. But as every prosecutor, defense attorney, and judge knows, the costs of a capital case begin long before the sentence is carried out. Experienced prosecutors and defense attorneys must be assigned and begin a long period of investigation and pre-trial hearings. Jury selection, the trial itself, and initial appeals will consume years of time and enormous amounts of money before an execution is on the horizon.

The Costs of the Death Penalty

The death penalty is an exceedingly expensive part of the criminal justice system because it is necessarily very inefficient. I say "necessarily" because, as the U.S. Supreme Court has repeatedly said when it comes to punishment, "death is different." This means that the ordinary system of due process is insufficient in capital cases. Virtually every step in the criminal justice process will take longer in a death penalty case and be more complicated. In terms of costs, it means that whatever expenses there are in an ordinary criminal case, they will be much higher in a capital case. More experienced lawyers

Richard C. Dieter, "Testimony of Richard C. Dieter, Executive Director, Death Penalty Information Center," Nebraska Judiciary Committee, March 13, 2013. Copyright © 2013 by Death Penalty Information Center. All rights reserved. Reproduced by permission.

will be needed, more experts will be employed, more questions will be asked of potential jurors, more time will be taken for the trial and appeals. The end result is that very few of the people selected for death penalty prosecution will ever be executed. And yet, the costs of every one of those potential cases must be counted to arrive at the true cost of the death penalty.

The cost of our country's going to the moon cannot be restricted to the expense of a single rocket and lander. We have to include all the experimental flights, all the research, all the failures and partial successes that necessarily precede such a complicated venture. The same is true for the death penalty. A typical state has hundreds of cases that are eligible for the death penalty. A formal capital prosecution will be undertaken in less than half of these cases; much fewer will go to trial; only some will be sentenced to death; and very, very few will survive appeals and result in an execution. Nebraska is a good example. According to an article in the *Omaha World-Herald*, during a period of almost 35 years after the death penalty was reinstated in 1973, 205 murder cases were eligible for the death penalty; 31 of those resulted in death sentences; and just 3 resulted in executions, though none since 1997. The extra costs of the death penalty were present in all of the cases where the prospect of the death penalty was raised, even in cases in which the death penalty was sought but a life sentence was given. Across the country, only about 15% of those who have been sentenced to death have been executed.

[The] costs reflect the reality that most capital prosecutions never result in a death sentence, and most death sentences do not result in an execution.

There is no national figure for the cost of the death penalty. Every state study is dependent on that state's laws, pay scales, and the extent to which it uses the death penalty. Studies have been conducted by research organizations, public defender offices, legislative committees, and the media. Researchers have employed different approaches, using different assumptions. However, *all of the studies conclude that the death penalty system is far more expensive than an alternative system in which the maximum sentence is life in prison.*

Some recent cost studies provide an example of how much the death penalty can cost over the years that the policy is in existence:

- In Maryland, a comprehensive cost study by the Urban Institute in 2008 estimated the extra costs to taxpayers for death penalty cases prosecuted between 1978 and 1999 to be $186 million. Based on the 5 executions carried out in the state, this translates to a cost of $37 million per execution. The complete cost of a death sentence (trial, appeals, incarceration on death row) was estimated to be $3 million. The cost for a comparable case in which death was not sought was $1.1 million (including life-time incarceration). (The state is on the verge of abolishing the death penalty.)

- In New York and New Jersey, the high costs of capital punishment were one factor in those states' decisions to abandon the death penalty. New York spent about $170 million over 9 years and had no executions. New Jersey spent $253 million over a 25-year period and also had no executions. In such states the cost per execution obviously cannot be calculated, but even assuming they eventually reached one execution every other year, and continued the annual expenditures indicated in their studies, the cost per execution would be in the $20-to-$40 million range.

- In 2008, the California Commission on the Fair Administration of Justice released an exhaustive report on the state's capital punishment system. The report found that the state was spending $137 million per year on the death penalty. The Commission estimated a comparable system that sentenced the same inmates to a maximum punishment of life without parole would cost only $11.5 million per year. Since the number of executions in California has averaged less than one every two years since the death penalty was reinstated in 1977, the cost *for each execution* is over $250 million. The state has also indicated it needs another $400 million to construct a new death row.

The death penalty cost California $90 million annually beyond the ordinary expenses of the justice system, of which $78 million was incurred at the trial level.

It is important to emphasize the high costs per execution do not mean that executions themselves are expensive, or that pursuing one execution will cost tens of millions of dollars. Rather, these costs reflect the reality that most capital prosecutions never result in a death sentence, and most death sentences do not result in an execution.

Death Penalty Costs Are Increasing

The costs of the death penalty when measured per execution are rising. In 1988, the *Miami Herald* estimated that the costs of the death penalty in Florida were $3.2 million per execution, based on the costs and rate of executions at that time. But today there are more people on death row, fewer executions per year, and higher overall costs, all contributing to a significantly *higher cost per execution*. A recent estimate by the *Palm Beach Post* found a much higher cost per execution: Florida now spends $51 million a year over what it would spend to punish all first-degree murderers with life in prison without parole. Based on the 44 executions Florida carried out from 1976 to 2000, that amounts to a cost of $24 million for each execution, a significant rise from earlier projections.

A similar increase appears in California. In 1988, the *Sacramento Bee* found that the death penalty cost California $90 million annually beyond the ordinary expenses of the justice system, of which $78 million was incurred at the trial level. But the costs have increased sharply since then. As noted above, the costs now are estimated at $137 million per year.

It is also revealing to examine the costs of specific features of the death penalty system, as revealed through state and federal studies:

- In Maryland, the 106 cases in which a death sentence was sought but *not imposed* will cost the state $71 million. This extra cost is solely due to the fact that the death penalty was pursued, even though the ultimate outcome was a life or long-term prison sentence.

- The average cost for just the *defense* at trial in a federal death case is $620,932, about 8 times that of a non-capital federal murder case.

- In Kansas, the *trial costs* for death cases were about 16 times greater than for non-death cases ($508,000 for death case; $32,000 for non-death case). The appeal costs for death cases were 21 times greater.

- In California, the *cost of confining one inmate to death, row* is $90,000 per year more than the costs of incarcerating the same inmate in a maximum-security prison. Death row inmates require higher security, often in single cells, where meals and other essentials are brought to them daily. This is a very inefficient means of confinement. With California's current death row population of over 700, that amounts to at least $63 million annually.

The Opportunity Costs of Death Penalty Cases

Generally, offices involved in the prosecution or defense of criminal cases expand or contract according to the work that must be done. The extra time required by death penalty cases typically has caused the size and budgets of such offices to increase, but not every cost associated with the death penalty appears as a line item in the state budget. Prosecutors, who are not paid by the hour, have been reluctant to divulge the time and related expenses reflecting their part in capital cases. Judges and public defenders are usually salaried employees who will be paid the same amount whether assigned to death penalty cases or other work. But a study would be incomplete if it did not include the *extra time* that pursuing the death penalty takes compared to cases prosecuted without the death penalty in calculating costs.

Whatever savings are produced through [plea bargaining] are overwhelmed by the costs of preparing for a death penalty prosecution, even if it never goes to trial.

If it takes 1,000 hours of state-salaried work to arrive at a death sentence and only 100 hours to have the same person sentenced to life without parole, the 900 hours difference is a state asset. If the death penalty is eliminated, the county or the state can decide whether to direct those employee-hours to other work that had been left undone, perhaps to pursue cold cases, or choose to keep fewer employees. There is a financial dimension to all aspects of death penalty cases, and proper cost studies take these "opportunity costs" into account.

The Effect of Plea Bargaining

One asserted refutation that has been offered to the high cost of the death penalty is that the threat of this punishment produces financial savings because defendants are more likely to accept plea bargains, thus avoiding the cost of a trial. However, whatever savings are produced through this ethically questionable practice are overwhelmed by the costs of preparing for a death penalty prosecution, even if it never goes to trial.

Some of the most thorough cost analyses conducted over the past 15 years specifically address plea bargaining as an area that could affect the costs of the death penalty, including those in North Carolina, Indiana, Kansas, and California, though some considered it too speculative to measure. These studies nevertheless concluded that the death penalty added significantly to the costs of the criminal justice system.

The dubiousness of any savings from this practice is underscored by a federal death penalty cost study. The Judicial Conference of United States concluded that the average cost of representation in federal death penalty cases *that resulted in plea bargains* was $192,333. The average cost of representation in cases that were eligible for the death penalty but in which the *death penalty was not sought* was only $55,772. This indicates that *seeking* the death penalty raises costs, even when the case results in a plea bargain. It would be far cheaper to pursue murder cases if the death penalty were never on the table, even taking some non-capital cases to trial, than to threaten the use of the death penalty to induce a plea bargain because the legal costs of preparing for a death penalty case far exceed the costs of a non-death penalty trial.

It is not just the price tag of the death penalty that has drawn concern, but rather what is society getting back from capital punishment for all the millions of dollars invested?

Moreover, data from some states refute the notion that the death penalty increases the incentive to plea bargain. Prosecutors in New Jersey said that abolition of the death penalty there in 2007 has made no difference in their ability to secure guilty pleas. In Alaska, where plea bargaining was abolished in 1975, a study by the National Institute of Justice found that since the end of plea bargaining, "guilty pleas continued to flow in at nearly undiminished rates. Most defendants pled guilty even when the state offered them nothing in exchange for their cooperation."

In addition, the practice of charging the death penalty for the purpose of obtaining plea bargains is an unethical and unconstitutional interference with a defendant's Sixth Amendment right to trial. It risks convicting innocent defendants who plead guilty solely to avoid the possibility of a death sentence—which has occurred on numerous occasions, including in Nebraska.

Some have argued that a consideration of costs has no place in our pursuit of justice. However, it is not just the price tag of the death penalty that has drawn concern, but rather what is society getting back from capital punishment for all the millions of dollars invested? And where else could that money be spent that might produce a greater benefit? The primary purpose of the criminal justice system is to make society safer. All aspects of this system—preventing crime, apprehending offenders, trials, and punishment—have costs. Cutbacks in any part of the criminal justice system can potentially result in a less safe society. Choices have to be made. The death penalty is the most expensive part of the system on a per-offender basis. Millions are spent seeking to achieve a single death sentence that, even if imposed is unlikely to be carried out. Money the police desperately need for more effective law enforcement is wasted on the death penalty. . . .

The Time Taken for Death Penalty Cases

Much of the delay in carrying out the death penalty is a healthy caution resulting from the near executions of innocent people. It is also the result of years of a very broad use of capital punishment, which created large death rows and a backlog of cases in the appellate courts.

For executions carried out in 2010, the average time between sentencing and execution was 15 years, the longest time for any year since the death penalty was reinstated in 1976. Even in Texas, the time between sentencing and execution is ten years. In some states, inmates are on death row for 20 or even 30 years awaiting execution. About 275 inmates have been on death row for 24 years or more.

In most states, executions are rare, the delay between sentencing and executions has lengthened, and the cost of death penalty cases has grown considerably.

This extensive delay results in the imposition of two sentences on the defendant: a life sentence in highly restricted confinement, *and* a death sentence. Of the capital cases that have been concluded, only about one-quarter of those sentenced to death were executed. Three-quarters of the defendants were permanently removed from death row for other reasons.

Such a system is enormously expensive for the state and a source of frustration for many. Death penalty cases are very costly to prosecute and defend compared to similar cases without the death penalty. When a death sentence is handed down, there will be years of expensive appeals and a form of incarceration that is much more expensive than the costs in general population. And at the end of the process, most defendants will end up with a life sentence anyhow—though one achieved through the most expensive process in the criminal justice system—the death penalty. Those left with a death sentence will probably not be the worst offenders, but rather an unfortunate few determined by arbitrary factors. Even for many supporters of capital punishment, this system makes little sense.

It has also created skepticism among the public regarding the value of such a nebulous form of justice. Indeed, some family members have remarked that, given the extensive time, the unpredictability of the outcome, and the painful re-living of the tragedy that inevitably accompanies this process, it would have been better if a life sentence had been imposed in the first place. . . .

The death penalty in the United States has become unwieldy. In most states, executions are rare, the delay between sentencing and executions has lengthened, and the cost of death penalty cases has grown considerably. Yet for all this additional effort, death penalty cases are still prone to error and the risk of executing an innocent person remains. The public and the families of victims have a right to be frustrated with this system. But there is no simple way to reduce delays and costs while ensuring that innocent lives are protected and that the system works fairly. This dilemma is one of the principal reasons that the use of the death penalty has declined so dramatically in recent years.

CHAPTER 3

Is the Death Penalty
Applied Fairly?

Overview: Death Penalty Demographics

Tracy L. Snell

Tracy L. Snell is a statistician for the Bureau of Justice Statistics within the US Department of Justice.

At year-end 2012, 35 states and the Federal Bureau of Prisons held 3,033 inmates under sentence of death, which was 32 fewer than at year-end 2011. This represents the twelfth consecutive year in which the number of inmates under sentence of death decreased.

Prisoners with Death Sentences

Four states (California, Florida, Texas, and Pennsylvania) held more than half of all inmates on death row on December 31, 2012. The Federal Bureau of Prisons held 56 inmates under sentence of death at year-end 2012.

Of prisoners under sentence of death at year-end 2012, 56% were white and 42% were black. The 384 Hispanic inmates under sentence of death accounted for 14% of inmates with a known ethnicity. Ninety-eight percent of inmates under sentence of death were male, and 2% were female. The race and sex of inmates under sentence of death has remained relatively unchanged since 2000.

Among inmates for whom legal status at the time of the capital offense was available, 40% had an active criminal justice status. About 4 in 10 of these inmates were on parole, and nearly 3 in 10 were on probation. The remaining inmates had charges pending, were incarcerated, had escaped from incarceration, or had some other criminal justice status.

Tracy L. Snell, "Capital Punishment, 2012—Statistical Tables," Bureau of Justice Statistics, no. NCJ 245789, May, 2014, pp. 1–2.

Criminal history patterns of death row inmates differed by race and Hispanic origin. More black inmates had a prior felony conviction (73%), compared to Hispanic (64%) or white (63%) inmates. Similar percentages of white (9%), black (9%), and Hispanic (6%) inmates had a prior homicide conviction. A slightly higher percentage of Hispanic (32%) and black (30%) inmates were on probation or parole at the time of their capital offense, compared to 24% of white inmates.

The Death Penalty in 2012

In 2012, 19 states and the Federal Bureau of Prisons reported that 79 inmates were received under sentence of death. Admissions in Florida (20), California (13), Texas (9), and Pennsylvania (6) accounted for 61% of those sentenced to death in 2012.

The number of inmates received in 2012 was the smallest number of admissions to death row since 1973 when 44 persons were admitted.

Twenty states and the Federal Bureau of Prisons removed 111 inmates from under sentence of death: 43 were executed, 17 died by means other than execution, and 51 were removed as a result of commutations or courts overturning sentences or convictions. Removals in Texas (17) and Florida (10) accounted for a quarter of all inmates removed from under sentence of death in 2012.

Nine states executed 43 inmates in 2012. The inmates executed in 2012 had been under sentence of death an average of 15 years and 10 months, which was 8 months less than those executed in 2011.

Among the 36 jurisdictions with prisoners under sentence of death at year-end 2012, 5 jurisdictions had more inmates than at year-end 2011, 13 had fewer inmates, and 18 had the same number. Florida showed the largest increase (up 10 inmates). Oklahoma and Texas (down 8 each), followed by Mississippi (down 7), North Carolina (down 6), and Arizona (down 5) had the largest decreases.

The Death Penalty in Recent Decades

The U.S. Supreme Court reinstated the death penalty in 1976. From 1976 to 2000, the number of inmates under sentence of death in the U.S. steadily increased until it peaked at 3,601 inmates on December 31, 2000. In 2001, the number of inmates removed from under sentence of death was higher than the number admitted for the first time since 1976. The number of annual removals of those under sentence of death exceeded the number of admissions every year since 2001. The 79 inmates received under sentence of death in 2012 represent a 5% decrease from the 83 inmates received in 2011. The number of inmates received in 2012 was the smallest number of admissions to death row since 1973 when 44 persons were admitted.

Of the 8,032 people under sentence of death between 1977 and 2012, 16% had been executed, 6% died by causes other than execution, and 40% received other dispositions. The federal government began collecting annual execution statistics in 1930. Between 1930 and 2012, a total of 5,179 inmates were executed under civil authority. After the Supreme Court reinstated death penalty statutes in 1976, 35 states and the federal government executed 1,320 inmates.

Disparity in
Death Penalty Rates Is Not
Evidence of Racial Bias

Kent S. Scheidegger

Kent S. Scheidegger is the legal director of the Criminal Justice Legal Foundation.

Opponents of the death penalty speak breathlessly of "disparities" in the application of the death penalty. In its broadest sense, "disparity" simply means that someone compiled some numbers and found that some rate differs among ethnic groups or among localities. Of course rates differ. The country and the state are heterogeneous. Crime rates vary. The extent to which witnesses are willing to come forward varies. Many factors vary. A mere difference in raw data is not proof that invidious racial discrimination is the cause of the difference. It should not even be considered as evidence of such discrimination. Disparity is evidence of discrimination only when a careful analysis of cases rules out legitimate reasons for the difference. . . .

The word "discriminate" has negative connotations from its association with racial discrimination, but in its core meaning "discriminate" simply means "To make a clear distinction; distinguish. . . . To make sensible decisions; judge wisely." The Supreme Court's requirement of individualized sentencing is a requirement that sentencers "discriminate" on the basis of legitimate factors that distinguish the more culpable murderers from those that are less so. When the legitimate

Kent S. Scheidegger, "Mend It, Don't End It: A Report to the Connecticut General Assembly on Capital Punishment," Criminal Justice Legal Foundation, April, 2011, pp. 14–24. Copyright © 2011 by Kent S. Scheidegger. All rights reserved. Reproduced by permission.

factors happen to correlate with illegitimate factors, the raw data on demographics tell us nothing.

Studies in this area attempt to cope with this problem by examining case files for the legitimate factors and developing mathematical models to adjust for them. The problem is that the legitimate factors cannot be fully known from the case files, and the studies never include all the legitimate factors even when they are discernable. For example, the model from the Baldus Georgia study primarily used by the petitioner in the *McCleskey* case was held to be invalid by the Federal District Court because (among other deficiencies) it failed to account for the strength of the prosecution's case for guilt. Prosecutors certainly should be more reluctant to seek the death penalty when the case for guilt is less than airtight, and juries certainly should be more reluctant to impose it when they have lingering doubt. . . .

The Race of the Defendant

By far, the type of potential discrimination of greatest concern is discrimination against racial minority defendants on the basis of their race. This form alone, of all the disparities commonly discussed, would, if true, mean that people are on death row who do not deserve to be there. (The others are discussed below.) Discrimination against black defendants was the great concern looming in the background when the Supreme Court threw out the then-existing death penalty laws in 1972 [in *Furman v. Georgia*].

Fortunately, nearly all the studies of post-1972 capital sentencing show no evidence of race-of-defendant bias. This result is particularly striking given that many of the studies are conducted or sponsored by opponents of capital punishment for the specific purpose of attacking it. While a study result that supports a sponsor's argument should be regarded with suspicion, a result that contradicts the sponsor's argument conversely warrants special confidence. The authors [David C.

Baldus, Charles Pulaski, and George Woodworth] of the best known of these studies, the Baldus study in Georgia, noted, "What is most striking about these results is the total absence of any race-of-defendant effect." This result has been repeated many times in many jurisdictions, including New Jersey, Maryland, Nebraska, Virginia, and the federal system. As in any field of study, there are some outliers. Overall, though, this result is sufficiently consistent that even a prominent death penalty opponent [Virginia Sloan] concedes, "It's not the race of the defendant that is the major factor, and I don't think there are many studies that claim that."

"Disparity" is not a defect; it is a virtue.

The result in Connecticut follows the national pattern. A study commissioned by an opponent—the Public Defender—concluded flatly, "There was no evidence that the defendant's race was related to procedural and sentencing advancement." Decades of the most strenuous searching for race-of-defendant bias in the post-1972 era has come up empty. This is a success to be celebrated. The post-*Furman* reforms worked.

With the most salient form of discrimination unsupported by their own studies, opponents of the death penalty turned to more esoteric forms. These include the claimed "race-of-victim bias" and "geographic disparity." We will take them in reverse order, because it is necessary to understand the geographic effect in order to understand the true cause of the numbers claimed to support "race-of-victim bias."

The Charge of Geographic "Disparity"

In America, government power and decision making are divided among many levels and many independent branches of government, more so than in any other country. This division is by design, not by accident, and it is an essential part of the genius of the American system. Indeed, one of the reasons we still have the death penalty in most of the United States, while elitists have repealed it over the objections of the people in many other countries, is because our divided-power structure keeps the government more responsive to the wishes of the people.

The fundamental question of whether the death penalty will be an available option for murder is decided at the state level. For the worst murders, the death penalty is available in Connecticut and New Hampshire but not in Massachusetts or Vermont. This is a "geographic disparity." This is also American federal democracy working as designed. The people of each of these states have chosen to have or not have the death penalty through the democratic process. The same is true of noncapital sentencing. The decision of how many years in prison are sufficient to punish rape, for example, is one the people of each state can make for themselves. "Disparity" is not a defect; it is a virtue.

The actual implementation of the criminal law is, to a large extent, delegated further down to the local level. In almost every state, prosecutors are elected by county or local district. Even more importantly, juries are selected locally. A jury of the "vicinage" is considered an important component of the constitutional right of trial by jury. The jury is expected to represent the "conscience of the community," not the conscience of the state.

When decisions are made that involve the exercise of discretion, different people will necessarily make different decisions in some cases, particularly the close cases. Local selection of decision-makers necessarily results in variation among localities. This happens all the time in noncapital cases. If a homicide is on the ragged edge between murder and manslaughter, a prosecutor in one jurisdiction may offer a plea bargain to manslaughter that would not be offered in another, or juries in the two localities might come in with different verdicts after trial of similar cases. There is no wailing and gnashing of teeth over these variations in noncapital cases. They are an understood and accepted product of local control.

Even if the claim [of racial bias] were valid, then, it would not be an argument for doing away with the death penalty.

The death penalty is for the worst murders and murderers, but "worst" cannot be mechanically defined. Distinguishing the worst from the not-quite-worst is necessarily a matter of discretion. We should not be surprised if an urban community jaded by chronic violence defines the worst murders more restrictively than a community where violence is comparatively rare. As with other "geographic disparities," this is not a defect; it is local control working as designed. Among the most thorough analyses in this area is by Judge David Baime, appointed as a special master by the Supreme Court of New Jersey. What he concluded could just as easily be said of Connecticut:

> New Jersey is a small and densely populated state. It is, nevertheless, a heterogenous one. It is thus not remarkable that the counties do not march in lockstep in the manner in which death-eligible cases are prosecuted.

The 2003 Connecticut Study proceeds on the premise that geographic variation is judicially suspect. That is a fundamentally erroneous premise. Geographic variation is a normal and proper product of local elections and juries of the vicinage in the American criminal justice system.

The Race of the Victim

Ever since the Baldus study in Georgia in the 1980s, the primary discrimination claim has been that the death penalty is imposed less often when the victim is black. Even if that were true, it would not mean that a single person is on death row who does not deserve to be there. The race-neutral benchmark for which cases deserve the death penalty is set in cases where race is not a factor, *i.e.*, where the perpetrator, victim, and principal decision-makers are all the same race. In practice, in most of American society traditionally, that has meant when they are all white. If the death penalty is imposed less often when the victim is black, that means that there are perpetrators in black-victim cases who should have been sentenced to death but were not. The unjustly lenient sentences in such a hypothetical case cannot, in any event, be corrected with unjust leniency in another case. Even if the claim were valid, then, it would not be an argument for doing away with the death penalty. It would be an argument for redoubling efforts to obtain death sentences in black-victim cases where the sentence is warranted.

When murder is more common, people tend to become jaded and less easily shocked.

The claim is not valid, though. Time after time, when the data are properly analyzed and confounding factors properly controlled, the claimed race-of-victim bias has vanished into the statistical grass. . . .

The federal system has been the subject of a unique research effort in this regard. A release of raw data in 2000, making no attempt to control for legitimate case characteristics, had raised charges that there was a race-of-victim bias in the Department of Justice's decision to seek the death penalty. Following the gathering of data needed for proper controls, the analysis was assigned to three independent teams to determine whether the data really did indicate racial bias. The three independent teams came to consistent conclusions: "The disparities disappear when data in the AG's [Attorny General] case files are used to adjust for the heinousness of the crime."

Results of studies from other states are mostly consistent with the federal result. In California, a study by RAND Corporation found no evidence of discrimination based on either the race of the victim or the race of the defendant. In Nebraska, Baldus *et al.* found "no significant evidence of systemic disparate treatment on the basis of the race of the defendant or the race of the victim in either the major urban counties or the counties of greater Nebraska on the part of either the prosecutors or judges." In Maryland, when the apparent race-of-victim effect was controlled for jurisdiction, it disappeared at some points in the study, but a residual effect remained at other points.

The 2003 study in Connecticut is consistent with these results. As noted previously, there is no evidence of a race-of-defendant bias. The study found a relation between race of the victim and the intermediate step of proceeding to a penalty trial, but none with the important final result of a death sentence. The needed correction for the legitimate variable of jurisdiction could not be done because the sample size was too small. The information available therefore provides no reason to doubt that the situation in Connecticut is consistent with the overall national picture, *i.e.*, that claimed racial disparities would shrink to insignificance if legitimate factors, *including jurisdiction*, could properly be taken into account. . . .

The False Impression of Racial Bias

Why is it that more sparing use of the death penalty by jurisdiction correlates with race, such that statewide numbers give a false impression of racial bias that dissipates upon proper correction for jurisdiction? There are two obvious reasons. The first is the unpleasant but undeniable reality in America today that the urban centers with high black populations also tend to have higher crime rates and particularly higher murder rates. . . . When murder is more common, people tend to become jaded and less easily shocked.

The second reason is that opposition to capital punishment is much higher among black Americans than among any other demographic group. Over the past several decades, white Americans have favored the death penalty by overwhelming margins. Solid majorities are in favor among both Republicans and Democrats, both college graduates and those with high school or less, both young and old, and even liberals and conservatives. Black Americans alone, among all the groups tallied, have been about evenly divided, with relatively narrow majorities shifting between support and opposition.

What happens when a demographic group with unusually strong opposition to the death penalty comprises an unusually large proportion of the population in a particular locality? Charles Lane of the *Washington Post* notes,

> In jurisdictions with large African-American populations, where most black-on-black crime occurs, persuading a jury to sentence the defendant to death is relatively difficult.... Also, in jurisdictions where elected prosecutors must appeal to black voters, prosecutors are that much less likely to support capital punishment.
>
> This is how race-of-the-victim disparities can be said to reflect racial progress. After all, blacks neither voted in elections nor served on juries in substantial numbers, especially in the South, until the late 1960s. Now that they do, they appear to be using this power to limit capital punishment in the cases closest to them.

The NAACP's [National Association for the Advancement of Colored People] statement to the Judiciary Committee claims, "Statistics show time and again that the color of skin of victims is one of the most telling indicators of whether or not someone will get a death sentence." That is simply not true. What the statistics show, when properly analyzed, is that the NAACP and other opponents of the death penalty have succeeded in reducing the application of the death penalty within the communities with the highest black populations and the greatest numbers of black-victim murders.

For those of us who believe that the death penalty is appropriate for the worst murderers, this is not a good result. It is not, however, a product or an indication of racism.

In summary, there is no good reason to believe the claim that race is a predominant factor, or even a major factor, in determining which murderers are sentenced to death. What limited disparities may remain are not even close to a sufficient reason to abandon justice and settle for an inadequate, watered-down sentence for the worst murderers, whatever color they may be.

Justice After Troy Davis

Ross Douthat

Ross Douthat is an op-ed columnist for The New York Times.

It's easy to see why the case of Troy Davis, the Georgia man executed last week [September 21, 2011] for the 1989 killing of an off-duty police officer, became a cause célèbre for death penalty opponents. Davis was identified as the shooter by witnesses who later claimed to have been coerced by investigators. He was prosecuted and convicted based on the same dubious eyewitness testimony, rather than forensic evidence. And his appeals process managed to be ponderously slow without delivering anything like certainty: it took the courts 20 years to say a final no to the second trial that Davis may well have deserved.

The Concern About Innocence

For many observers, the lesson of this case is simple: We need to abolish the death penalty outright. The argument that capital punishment is inherently immoral has long been a losing one in American politics. But in the age of DNA evidence and endless media excavations, the argument that courts and juries are just too fallible to be trusted with matters of life and death may prove more effective.

If capital punishment disappears in the United States, it won't be because voters and politicians no longer want to execute the guilty. It will be because they're afraid of executing the innocent.

This is a healthy fear for a society to have. But there's a danger here for advocates of criminal justice reform. After all,

Ross Douthat, "Justice After Troy Davis," *New York Times*, September 25, 2011, p. SR16. Copyright © 2011 by New York Times Company. All rights reserved. Reproduced by permission.

in a world without the death penalty, Davis probably wouldn't have been retried or exonerated. His appeals would still have been denied, he would have spent the rest of his life in prison, and far fewer people would have known or cared about his fate.

The Importance of Scrutiny

Instead, he received a level of legal assistance, media attention and activist support that few convicts can ever hope for. And his case became an example of how the very finality of the death penalty can focus the public's attention on issues that many Americans prefer to ignore: the overzealousness of cops and prosecutors, the limits of the appeals process and the ugly conditions faced by many of the more than two million Americans currently behind bars.

The case for executing murderers is a case for proportionality in punishment: for sentences that fit the crime, and penalties that close the circle.

Simply throwing up our hands and eliminating executions entirely, by contrast, could prove to be a form of moral evasion—a way to console ourselves with the knowledge that no innocents are ever executed, even as more pervasive abuses go unchecked. We should want a judicial system that we can trust with matters of life and death, and that can stand up to the kind of public scrutiny that Davis's case received. And gradually reforming the death penalty—imposing it in fewer situations and with more safeguards, which other defendants could benefit from as well—might do more than outright abolition to address the larger problems with crime and punishment in America.

This point was made well last week by Pascal-Emmanuel Gobry, writing for *The American Scene*. In any penal system, he pointed out, but especially in our own—which can be brutal, overcrowded, rife with rape and other forms of violence—a lifelong prison sentence can prove more cruel and unusual than a speedy execution. And a society that supposedly values liberty as much or more than life itself hasn't necessarily become more civilized if it preserves its convicts' lives while consistently violating their rights and dignity. It's just become better at self-deception about what's really going on.

The Need for Genuine Justice

Fundamentally, most Americans who support the death penalty do so because they want to believe that our justice system is *just*, and not merely a mechanism for quarantining the dangerous in order to keep the law-abiding safe. The case for executing murderers is a case for proportionality in punishment: for sentences that fit the crime, and penalties that close the circle.

Instead of dismissing this point of view as backward and barbaric, criminal justice reformers should try to harness it, by pointing out that too often our punishments don't fit the crime—that sentences for many drug crimes are disproportionate to the offenses, for instance, or that rape and sexual assault have become an implicit part of many prison terms. Americans should be urged to support penal reform not in spite of their belief that some murderers deserve execution, in other words, but because of it—because both are attempts to ensure that accused criminals receive their just deserts.

Abolishing capital punishment in a kind of despair over its fallibility would send a very different message. It would tell the public that our laws and courts and juries are fundamentally incapable of delivering what most Americans consider genuine justice. It could encourage a more cynical and utilitarian view of why police forces and prisons exist, and what moral standards we should hold them to. And while it would put an end to wrongful executions, it might well lead to more overall injustice.

The US Death Penalty
Is Inseparable
from White Supremacy

Ta-Nehisi Coates

Ta-Nehisi Coates is a senior editor for The Atlantic.

Fifteen years ago, Clayton Lockett shot Stephanie Neiman twice, then watched as his friends buried her alive. Last week [April 29, 2014], Lockett was tortured to death by the state of Oklahoma. The torture was not so much the result of intention as neglect. The state knew that its chosen methods—a triple-drug cocktail—could result in a painful death. (An inmate executed earlier this year by the method was heard to say, "I feel my whole body burning.") Oklahoma couldn't care less. It executed Lockett anyway.

The Issue of Racial Bias

Over at *Bloomberg View*, Ramesh Ponnuru has taken the occasion to pen a column ostensibly arguing against the death penalty. But Ponnuru, evidently embarrassed to find himself in liberal company, spends most of the column dismissing the arguments of soft-headed bedfellows:

> On the core issue—yes or no on capital punishment—I'm with the opponents. Better to err on the side of not taking life. The teaching of the Catholic Church, to which I belong, seems right to me: The state has the legitimate authority to execute criminals, but it should refrain if it has other means of protecting people from them. Our government almost always does.

Ta-Nehisi Coates, "The Inhumanity of the Death Penalty," *Atlantic*, May 12, 2014. © 2014 The Atlantic Media Co., as first published in The Atlantic Magazine. All rights reserved. Distributed by Tribune Content Agency, LLC. Reproduced by permission.

Still, when I hear about an especially gruesome crime, like the one the Oklahoma killer committed, I can't help rooting for the death penalty. And a lot of the arguments its opponents make are unconvincing.

Take the claims of racial bias—that we execute black killers, or the killers of white victims, at disproportionate rates. Even if those disputed claims are true, they don't point toward abolition of the death penalty. Executing more white killers, or killers of black victims, would reduce any disparity just as well.

Well into the 20th century, capital punishment was, as John Locke would say, lynching "coloured with the name, pretences, or forms of law."

Indeed it would. But the reason we don't do this is contained within Ponnuru's inquiry: bias. When Ponnuru suggests that the way to correct for the death penalty's disproportionate use is to execute more white people, he is presenting a world in which the death penalty has neither history nor context. One merely flips the "Hey Guys, Let's Not Be Racist" switch and then the magic happens.

The History of White Supremacy

Those of us who cite the disproportionate application of the death penalty as a reason for outlawing it do so because we believe that a criminal-justice system is not an abstraction but a real thing, existing in a real context, with a real history. In America, the history of the criminal justice—and the death penalty—is utterly inseparable from white supremacy. During the Civil War, black soldiers were significantly more likely to be court-martialed and executed than their white counterparts. This practice continued into World War II. "African-Americans comprised 10 percent of the armed forces but accounted for almost 80 percent of the soldiers executed during the war," writes law professor Elizabeth Lutes Hillman.

In American imagination, the lynching era is generally seen as separate from capital punishment. But virtually no one was ever charged for lynching. The country refused to outlaw it. And sitting U.S. senators such as Ben Tillman and Theodore Bilbo openly called for lynching for crimes as grave as rape and as dubious as voting. Well into the 20th century, capital punishment was, as John Locke would say, lynching "coloured with the name, pretences, or forms of law."

The youngest American ever subjected to the death penalty was George Junius Stinney. It is very hard to distinguish his case from an actual lynching. At age 14, Stinney, a black boy, walked to the execution chamber

> with a Bible under his arm, which he later used as a booster seat in the electric chair. Standing 5 foot 2 inches (157 cm) tall and weighing just over 90 pounds (40 kg), his size (relative to the fully grown prisoners) presented difficulties in securing him to the frame holding the electrodes. Nor did the state's adult-sized face-mask fit him; as he was hit with the first 2,400 V surge of electricity, the mask covering his face slipped off, "revealing his wide-open, tearful eyes and saliva coming from his mouth. . . . After two more jolts of electricity, the boy was dead."

Living with racism in America means tolerating a level of violence inflicted on the black body that we would not upon the white body. This deviation is not a random fact, but the price of living in a society with a lengthy history of considering black people as a lesser strain of humanity. When you live in such a society, the prospect of incarcerating, disenfranchising, and ultimately executing white humans at the same rate as black humans makes makes very little sense. Disproportion is the point.

A Disturbing Logic

The "Hey Guys, Let's Not Be Racist" switch is really "Hey Guys, Let's Pretend We Aren't American" switch or a "Hey

Guys, Let's Pretend We Aren't Human Beings" switch. The death penalty—like all state actions—exists within a context constructed by humans, not gods. Humans tend to have biases, and the systems we construct often reflect those biases. Understanding this, it is worth asking whether our legal system should be in the business of doling out an ultimate punishment, one for which there can never be any correction. Citing racism in our justice system isn't mere shaming, it's a call for a humility and self-awareness, which presently evades us.

I was sad to see Ponnuru's formulation, because it so echoed the unfortunate thoughts of William F. Buckley. In 1965, Buckley debated James Baldwin at the Cambridge Union Society. That was the year John Lewis was beaten at the Edmund Pettus Bridge, and Viola Liuzzo was shot down just outside of Selma, Alabama. In that same campaign, Martin Luther King gave, arguably, his greatest speech. ("How Long? Not long. Truth forever on the scaffold. Wrong forever on the throne.") In whole swaths of the country, black people lacked the basic rights of citizenship—central among them, the right to vote. Buckley spent much of his time sneering at complaints of American racism. When the issue of the vote was raised Buckley responded by saying that the problem with Mississippi wasn't that "not enough Negroes have the vote but that too many white people are voting."

There's something revealed in the logic—in both Ponnuru and Buckley's case—that we should fix disproportion by making more white people into niggers. It is the same logic of voter-ID laws, which will surely disenfranchise huge swaths of white voters, for the goal of disenfranchising proportionally more black voters. I'm not sure what all that means—it's the shadow of something I haven't worked out.

The Death Penalty Is Carried Out Against Those with Mental Illness

Natasha Lennard

Natasha Lennard is a senior news analyst for Vice News.

In December 2008, Andre Thomas pulled out and ate his left eyeball. He had gouged out the right eye in 2004, having taken a bible passage literally, six days after he brutally murdered his estranged wife, their young son and her 13-month-old daughter. His attorney Maurie Levin, who is co-director of Texas' Capital Punishment Clinic, told *Salon* that her client is "transparently and floridly" mentally ill. He was diagnosed as schizophrenic while in prison, having heard voices in his head since childhood. What sort of system sentences Andre Thomas to death?

Mental Illness and Criminal Justice

Texas Tribune managing editor Brandi Grissom has followed Thomas' case closely. As she noted in an excellent feature for the *Texas Monthly*, "as he awaits execution, Andre and his tragic case force uncomfortable questions about the intersection of mental illness and the criminal justice system." Thomas is certainly not the only death row inmate to have been diagnosed with mental illness; more than 20 percent of the 290 inmates on Texas' death row are considered mentally ill, as Grissom noted. But the extremity of his situation has prompted fervid responses locally and nationally. "It's astonishing, just how many problems in the legal system [this case] exemplifies," said Levin in a phone interview.

Natasha Lennard, "A Schizophrenic Who Gouged Out His Eyes Is on Texas Death Row," February 25, 2013. This article first appeared in Salon.com, at http://www.Salon.com. An online version remains in the Salon archives. Reprinted with permission.

Who gets to be sane? Who gets to be accountable? Who gets to be executed?—Thomas, fully blind and heavily medicated, faces the death penalty as a limit case for Texas' answer to these problematic questions.

[Thomas] was deemed competent to stand trial—trial for capital murder at that—after he had already gouged out his eye and exhibited other psychotic tendencies.

To be sure, the crime for which Thomas was capitally charged was horrific. Grissom's account bears reprinting:

> By 2004, Andre was 21 years old, deeply mentally ill, and receiving no treatment. On the bright, clear morning of March 27, he charged up the stairs to the third-floor apartment where Laura [his estranged wife] lived and kicked in the door. Her boyfriend had already left for work. Andre was holding three knives, one for each of his intended victims. He first encountered Laura, who ran toward him, screaming "No!" Andre plunged a knife into her chest. He then reached in and pulled out what he believed was her heart (he had, in fact, extracted part of her lung). Next, he headed for the children's room, where Andre Jr. and 1-year-old Leyha were sleeping. Andre held down his 4-year-old son and stabbed him before moving on to Leyha. He carved out each of the children's hearts. Finally, Andre jammed a knife into his own chest three times and lay down beside Laura on the living room floor, expecting to die. Confounded when he didn't, he slipped the organs he had removed into his pocket and walked more than five miles home. A few hours later, he went to the Sherman Police Department, where he confessed to the murders and asked if he would be forgiven. "I thought it was what God wanted me to do," he later told investigators.

> After undergoing emergency surgery to repair his life-threatening stab wounds, Andre was moved to the Grayson County jail, where his behavior became more and more psy-

chotic. He gestured wildly and announced that he was going to save the world. He claimed to be "the thirteenth warrior on the dollar bill" and said that Laura and the children weren't dead but that their hearts had been freed from evil.

There is no correct procedure to deal with Andre Thomas. The questions of how someone ends up in such a tormented state—the conditions that make the above horrors possible—are far beyond the purview of this writing. We can say, however, that there are many profoundly wrong ways to deal with Andre Thomas—and these are the ways he has been dealt with.

> *The idea of justice at play here rests on a person being able to understand, in advance of their execution, why and for what they are being killed.*

Problems in the Case

Firstly, he was deemed competent to stand trial—trial for capital murder at that—after he had already gouged out his eye and exhibited other psychotic tendencies. While considered competent to be tried for a death sentence, it's worth noting that the Texas Department of Criminal Justice deemed him incompetent to speak with a journalist. As Grissom wrote, while she was permitted to tour the psychiatric facility currently holding Thomas, [she] was not allowed to speak with him. "John Hurt, a spokesman for the department, explained that the policy is meant to protect inmates 'who may not be mentally competent to sit for an interview.' It was a remarkable response given that Andre had already been deemed competent for trial and is currently considered competent to be executed," wrote Grissom.

But this is just one of many paradoxes and absurdities characterizing Thomas' treatment—among them the fact that the Texas Court of Criminal Appeals found the defendant "clearly 'crazy' but . . . also 'sane' under Texas law."

Undergirding the case is the problem of racism in the criminal justice system. Thomas, a young African American man in a small town in Texas was tried in front of an all white jury for the murder of a white woman. Four jurors, Levin told *Salon*, had written on a questionnaire that they objected to interracial relationships. According to the attorney and legal scholar, the prosecutor went on a "soliloquy . . . invoking race based fears" about the defendant "getting out and dating your daughters."

Thomas was sentenced to death and—like all those so condemned—was confined to a six-by-10 ft. cell for 23 hours a day. The facility, says Levin, showed "shocking inadequacy" in dealing with Thomas' mental deterioration. There, the convicted man gouged out his other eye and rendered himself fully blind. Thomas and his legal team currently await the decision of a federal court on whether he is sane enough to be executed.

As a limit case, Thomas highlights the juridical determinations around the right to life: What are the conditions necessary for the state to kill a person? The arguments in Thomas' first capital murder trial fell around whether the killer knew right from wrong at the time of carrying out the murders. Now, the terrain of debate has shifted to whether Thomas is competent enough to comprehend his own capital punishment. Levin argues that her client lacks any such rational understanding and that, although treated with anti-psychotic medicines, he still hears voices, she said.

The Legal Framework

The entire legal framework is troubling. The idea of justice at play here rests on a person being able to understand, in advance of their execution, why and for what they are being killed. Grissom cites Thurgood Marshall's 1986 majority SCOTUS [Supreme Court of the United States] opinion on the issue of executing the mentally ill, which set up the current legal standard: "We may seriously question the retributive value of executing a person who has no comprehension of why he has been singled out and stripped of his fundamental right to life," wrote Justice Marshall. While, of course, many of us would also vehemently challenge the retributive value of the state executing persons with full comprehension of why they have been so singled out to face death, it seems clear that Marshall's "comprehension" condition sets up profound problems when it comes to the mentally ill.

When it comes to the intellectually disabled (referred to in U.S. law as "mentally retarded") the story is slightly different. The Supreme Court has ruled that the "mentally retarded," as well as juveniles, cannot be held to the same standards of culpability as most adults and thus the death penalty in such cases would violate the constitution's ban on cruel and unusual punishment. Of course, even in cases of proven mental disability, death sentences are still carried out. The state of Georgia, for example, is currently pushing to have a stay of execution removed in the case of 38-year-old Warren Hill, a death row inmate found mentally retarded by physicians. Mental illness—where there is sometimes possibility of medicating a prisoner into a state of execution-worthy comprehension—brings up even more troubling grey areas for capital sentencing.

Levin told *Salon* that there is a "deficit in forums to even discuss how to redress the issues this case raises." If the case of Andre Thomas—schizophrenic, self-blinded and facing death by the state—doesn't urge the importance of such forums, it's hard to imagine what might.

Innocent People Are Given Death Sentences

Samuel R. Gross et al.

Samuel R. Gross coauthored the following viewpoint with Barbara O'Brien, Chen Hu, and Edward H. Kennedy. Gross is the Thomas and Mabel Long Professor of Law at the University of Michigan Law School. O'Brien is associate professor of law at Michigan State University College of Law. Hu and Kennedy are biostatisticians at the American College of Radiology Clinical Research Center and the University of Pennsylvania School of Medicine, respectively.

In the past few decades a surge of hundreds of exonerations of innocent criminal defendants has drawn attention to the problem of erroneous conviction, and led to a spate of reforms in criminal investigation and adjudication. All the same, the most basic empirical question about false convictions remains unanswered: How common are these miscarriages of justice?

Estimating False Convictions

False convictions, by definition, are unobserved when they occur: If we know that a defendant is innocent, he is not convicted in the first place. They are also extremely difficult to detect after the fact. As a result, the great majority of innocent defendants remain undetected. The rate of such errors is often described as a "dark figure"—an important measure of the performance of the criminal justice system that is not merely unknown but unknowable.

Samuel R. Gross, Barbara O'Brien, Chen Hu, and Edward H. Kennedy, "Rate of False Conviction of Criminal Defendants Who Are Sentenced to Death," PNAS, April 28, 2014, pp. 1–2, 5–6. Copyright © 2014 by PNAS. All rights reserved. Reproduced by permission.

However, there is no shortage of lawyers and judges who assert confidently that the number of false convictions is negligible. Judge Learned Hand said so in 1923: "Our [criminal] procedure has always been haunted by the ghost of the innocent man convicted. It is an unreal dream." And in 2007, Justice Antonin Scalia wrote in a concurring opinion in the Supreme Court that American criminal convictions have an "error rate of [0].027 percent—or, to put it another way, a success rate of 99.973 percent." This would be comforting, if true. In fact, the claim is silly. Scalia's ratio is derived by taking the number of known exonerations at the time, which were limited almost entirely to a small subset of murder and rape cases, using it as a measure of all false convictions (known and unknown), and dividing it by the number of all felony convictions for all crimes, from drug possession and burglary to car theft and income tax evasion.

The vast majority of criminal convictions are not candidates for exoneration because no one makes any effort to reconsider the guilt of the defendants.

To actually estimate the proportion of erroneous convictions we need a well-defined group of criminal convictions within which we identify all mistaken convictions, or at least most. It is hard to imagine how that could be done for criminal convictions generally, but it might be possible for capital murder.

The Exoneration Rate

The rate of exonerations among death sentences in the United States is far higher than for any other category of criminal convictions. Death sentences represent less than one-tenth of 1% of prison sentences in the United States, but they accounted for about 12% of known exonerations of innocent defendants from 1989 through early 2012, a disproportion of more than 130 to 1. A major reason for this extraordinary exoneration rate is that far more attention and resources are devoted to death penalty cases than to other criminal prosecutions, before and after conviction.

The vast majority of criminal convictions are not candidates for exoneration because no one makes any effort to reconsider the guilt of the defendants. Approximately 95% of felony convictions in the United States are based on negotiated pleas of guilty (plea bargains) that are entered in routine proceedings at which no evidence is presented. Few are ever subject to any review whatsoever. Most convicted defendants are never represented by an attorney after conviction, and the appeals that do take place are usually perfunctory and unrelated to guilt or innocence.

The proportion of death-sentenced inmates who are exonerated understates the rate of false convictions among death sentences because the intensive search for possible errors is largely abandoned once the threat of execution is removed.

Death sentences are different. Almost all are based on convictions after jury trial, and even the handful of capital defendants who plead guilty are then subject to trial-like-sentencing hearings, usually before juries. All death sentences are reviewed on appeal; almost all are reviewed repeatedly. With few exceptions, capital defendants have lawyers as long as they remain on death row. Everyone, from the first officer on the scene of a potentially capital crime to the Chief Justice of the United States, takes capital cases more seriously than other criminal prosecutions—and knows that everybody else will do so as well. And everyone from defense lawyers to innocence projects to governors and state and federal judges is likely to be particularly careful to avoid the execution of innocent defendants.

This extraordinary difference in resources and attention generates two related effects. (*i*) Advocates for a defendant are much more likely to pursue any plausible postconviction claim of innocence if the defendant is under sentence of death. (*ii*) Courts (and other government actors) are much more likely to consider and grant such a claim if the defendant is at risk for execution. As a result, false convictions are far more likely to be detected among those cases that end in death sentences than in any other category of criminal convictions.

A Better Estimate

The high exoneration rate for death sentences suggests that a substantial proportion of innocent defendants who are sentenced to death are ultimately exonerated, perhaps a majority. If so, we can use capital exonerations as a basis for estimating a lower bound for the false conviction rate among death sentences.

Since 1973, when the first death penalty laws now in effect in the United States were enacted, 143 death-sentenced defendants have been exonerated, from 1 to 33 y after conviction (mean = 10.1 y). In a previous study we found that 2.3% of all death sentences imposed from 1973 through 1989 resulted in exoneration by the end of 2004. A study by [Michael] Risinger estimated that had biological samples been available for testing in all cases, 3.3% of defendants sentenced to death between 1982 and 1989 for murders that included rape would have been exonerated by DNA evidence through February 2006. That estimate, however, is based on a small number of exonerations ($n = 11$). Both studies were limited to convictions that occurred 15 y or more before the study date, and so include a high proportion of all exonerations that will ever occur in the relevant groups. Nonetheless both studies underestimate the false conviction rate for death-sentenced defendants because they do not reflect exonerations that occur after the study period, and do not include false convictions that are never detected at all.

Capital defendants who are removed from death row but not exonerated—typically because their sentences are reduced to life imprisonment—no longer receive the extraordinary level of attention that is devoted to death row inmates. (This applies as well to those who are executed or die on death row from other causes.) If they are in fact innocent, they are much less likely to be exonerated than if they had remained on death row. As a result, the proportion of death-sentenced inmates who are exonerated understates the rate of false convictions among death sentences because the intensive search for possible errors is largely abandoned once the threat of execution is removed.

In other words, the engine that produces an exoneration rate that is a plausible proxy for the rate of false conviction among death-sentenced prisoners is the process of reinvestigation and reconsideration under threat of execution. Over time, most death-sentenced inmates are removed from death row and resentenced to life in prison—at which point their chances of exoneration appear to drop back to the background rate for all murders, or close to it. Thus, we will get a better estimate of the rate of false capital convictions if [we] are able to estimate "what the rate of capital exonerations would be if all death sentences were subject for an indefinite period to the level of scrutiny that applies to those facing the prospect of execution." This study does just that. . . .

The Number of Innocents

We present a conservative estimate of the proportion of erroneous convictions of defendants sentenced to death in the United States from 1973 through 2004, 4.1%. This is a unique finding; there are no other reliable estimates of the rate of false conviction in any context. The main source of potential bias is the accuracy of our classification of cases as true or false convictions. On that issue it is likely that we have an undercount, that there are more innocent death row defendants who have not been identified and exonerated than guilty ones who have been exonerated in error.

The most charged question in this area is different: How many innocent defendants have been put to death? We cannot estimate that number directly but we believe it is comparatively low. If the rate were the same as our estimate for false death sentences, the number of innocents executed in the United States in the past 35 y would be more than 50. We do not believe that has happened. Our data and the experience of practitioners in the field both indicate that the criminal justice system goes to far greater lengths to avoid executing innocent defendants than to prevent them from remaining in prison indefinitely. One way to do so is to disproportionately reverse death sentences in capital cases in which the accuracy of the defendants' convictions is in doubt and to resentence them to life imprisonment, a practice that makes our estimate of the rate of error conservative. However, no process of removing potentially innocent defendants from the execution queue can be foolproof. With an error rate at trial over 4%, it is all but certain that several of the 1,320 defendants executed since 1977 were innocent.

Most innocent defendants who have been sentenced to death have not been exonerated, and many—including the great majority of those who have been resentenced to life in prison—probably never will be.

It is possible that the death-sentencing rate of innocent defendants has changed over time. No specific evidence points in that direction, but the number and the distribution of death sentences have changed dramatically in the past 15 y. One change, however, is unlikely to have much impact: the advent of DNA identification technology. DNA evidence is useful primarily in rape rather than homicide investigations. Only 13% of death row exonerations since 1973 (18 of 142) resulted from postconviction DNA testing, so the availability of preconviction testing will have at most a modest effect on that rate.

Unfortunately, we cannot generalize from our findings on death sentences to the rate of false convictions in any broader category of crime. Capital prosecutions, and to a lesser extent murder cases in general, are handled very differently from other criminal cases. There are theoretical reasons to believe that the rate of false conviction may be higher for murders in general, and for capital murders in particular, than for other felony convictions, primarily because the authorities are more likely to pursue difficult cases with weak evidence of guilt if one or more people have been killed. However, there are no data that confirm or refute this hypothesis.

We do know that the rate of error among death sentences is far greater than Justice Scalia's reassuring 0.027%. That much is apparent directly from the number of death row exonerations that have already occurred. Our research adds the disturbing news that most innocent defendants who have been sentenced to death have not been exonerated, and many—including the great majority of those who have been resentenced to life in prison—probably never will be.

This is only part of a disturbing picture. Fewer than half of all defendants who are convicted of capital murder are ever sentenced to death in the first place. Sentencing juries, like other participants in the process, worry about the execution of innocent defendants. Interviews with jurors who participated in capital sentencing proceedings indicate that lingering doubts about the defendant's guilt is the strongest available predictor of a sentence of life imprisonment rather than death. It follows that the rate of innocence must be higher for convicted capital defendants who are not sentenced to death than for those who are. The net result is that the great majority of innocent defendants who are convicted of capital murder in the

United States are neither executed nor exonerated. They are sentenced, or resentenced to prison for life, and then forgotten.

How Should US Death Penalty Practices Be Reformed?

Overview: US Support for the Death Penalty

Pew Research Center

The Pew Research Center is a nonpartisan fact tank that informs the public about the issues, attitudes, and trends shaping America and the world.

According to a 2013 Pew Research Center survey, 55% of U.S. adults say they favor the death penalty for persons convicted of murder. A significant minority (37%) oppose the practice.

U.S. Support for the Death Penalty

While a majority of U.S. adults still support the death penalty, public opinion in favor of capital punishment has seen a modest decline since November 2011, the last time Pew Research asked the question. In 2011, fully six-in-ten U.S. adults (62%) favored the death penalty for murder convictions, and 31% opposed it.

Public support for capital punishment has ebbed and flowed over time, as indicated by polls going all the way back to the 1930s. But it has been gradually ticking downward for the past two decades, since Pew Research began collecting survey data on this issue. Since 1996, the margin between those who favor the death penalty and those who oppose it has narrowed from a 60-point gap (78% favor vs. 18% oppose) to an 18-point difference in 2013 (55% favor vs. 37% oppose).

Among most large U.S. religious groups, majorities support capital punishment. Roughly six-in-ten or more white

"Shrinking Majority of Americans Support Death Penalty," Pew Research Center, March 28, 2014, pp. 1–3. Reproduced by permission.

evangelical Protestants (67%), white mainline Protestants (64%) and white Catholics (59%) express support for the death penalty.

By contrast, black Protestants are more likely to say they oppose the death penalty than support it (58% vs. 33%), as are Hispanic Catholics (54% vs. 37%).

Even among white adults, support for capital punishment has decreased markedly over the past two decades.

Support Across Demographic Groups

The differences among religious groups reflect the overall racial and ethnic picture on support for capital punishment. Twice as many white Americans favor the death penalty as oppose it (63% vs. 30%). Among black adults, the balance of opinion is reversed: 55% oppose capital punishment, while 36% support it. The margin is narrower among Hispanics, but more oppose the death penalty (50%) than support it (40%).

Even among white adults, support for capital punishment has decreased markedly over the past two decades, from 81% in 1996 to 63% in 2013. Over the same time period, the share of blacks favoring the death penalty also has declined, from 55% to 36%.

About half or more of most demographic groups support capital punishment, with only modest differences among them.

Men are slightly more likely than women to say they favor the death penalty (58% vs. 52%). And Americans ages 50 and older are more likely than those under 50 to support capital punishment, by a similar margin (58% vs. 53%).

Politically, the differences are somewhat greater. Fully seven-in-ten Republicans (71%) express support for the death penalty, while roughly a quarter (23%) oppose it. Among Democrats, public opinion is more evenly divided: 45% are in favor of the death penalty for convicted murderers, and 47%

are opposed. Political independents fall in between the two parties, with 57% supporting capital punishment and 37% opposing it.

The Death Penalty Should Be Replaced by Life Without Parole

Lauren Galik

Lauren Galik is director of criminal justice reform at the Reason Foundation.

Last month [April 2014] condemned Oklahoma death row inmate Clayton Lockett was pronounced dead from an apparent heart attack more than 40 minutes after his botched execution had begun.

During that time, horrified eyewitnesses watched as Lockett writhed on the gurney, gasped, and even spoke after doctors had declared him unconscious.

This bungled execution has breathed new life into the debate over the death penalty, prompting other states to examine their own protocols and question whether or not capital punishment is worth the costs. California should be no exception.

The Death Penalty in California

There are 746 inmates on death row in California. Since the death penalty was reinstated in 1978, California has only executed 13 inmates.

Roughly seven times more death row inmates have died from natural causes, suicide, or were killed in other ways than have actually been executed in California. Nevertheless, California taxpayers have paid more than $4 billion to have the death penalty in the state according to a study published in the 2011 *Loyola of Los Angeles Law Review*.

Lauren Galik, "Time to Ditch the Death Penalty," *Orange County Register*, May 9, 2014. Copyright © 2014 by Reason Foundation. All rights reserved. Reproduced by permission.

The last time California executed a prisoner was in 2006. That same year, a federal judge halted all executions in California on the grounds that the state's three-drug lethal injection protocol risked causing inmates too much pain and suffering before death, which would be a violation of the Eighth Amendment of the Constitution.

In 2013, a California state appeals court scrapped the state's attempt to update its lethal injection procedures and California's death penalty has remained in limbo ever since.

Everything about the death penalty is significantly more expensive.

It's not just California that has faced problems with its lethal injection protocol, essentially experimental drugs from unknown sources, resulting in a number of legal challenges over the constitutionality of these drugs and protocols.

The Costs of the Death Penalty

Meanwhile, housing prisoners on death row continues to cost California taxpayers $184 million more per year than it would if those same prisoners had been sentenced to life in prison without the possibility of parole.

That's because everything about the death penalty is significantly more expensive.

According to the *Loyola of Los Angeles Law Review* study, the heightened security practices mandated for death row inmates cost more than $100,000 per prisoner every year. The state also pays up to $300,000 for attorneys to represent each capital case inmate during his or her appeals process.

What's more—the least expensive death penalty trial in the history of the state still cost $1.1 million more than the most expensive case seeking life without parole.

A Better Alternative

It's true that the prisoners on death row in California are often the worst of the worst offenders and deserve the most severe punishment for their crimes.

However, eliminating the death penalty and requiring them to serve the rest of their lives in prison without the possibility of parole would still guarantee that they would die behind bars.

If California abolished the death penalty, taxpayers wouldn't have to keep wasting billions of dollars on death row. The state could also avoid the controversy and legal challenges that would accompany a change to its lethal injection protocol.

And citizens could rest easy knowing that no innocent person will accidentally be put to death.

According to a new study in the scientific journal *Proceedings of the National Academy of Sciences*, 4 percent of offenders on death row in the United States are innocent.

With worries over innocent people who could be killed by the state, botched executions, experimental lethal injection drugs and concerns over the cost and effectiveness of the death penalty, the time is right for California to get rid of capital punishment for good.

Life Without Parole Is a Different Kind of Death Sentence

David R. Dow

David R. Dow is the Cullen Professor at the University of Houston Law Center and has defended over one hundred death row inmates in the past twenty years.

If you were sentenced to life in prison with no chance of release, how long would you want to live? Would you want to live at all?

Inmates on Death Row

I think about these questions often. My clients, inmates on death row, think about them every day. In more than twenty years of representing prisoners facing execution, I've had several ask me to waive their appeals so they could hurry up and die. There are some who think any client who "volunteers"— that's our euphemism for giving up—is necessarily irrational. I don't share that view. To be sure, two of my clients who told me to waive their appeals were mentally ill, and I fought to keep them from volunteering to die. But the others were perfectly rational. They did not want to spend at least six years, maybe fifteen, appealing their sentences, only to ultimately be strapped to a gurney and injected with poison.

It's easy for most people to see their decisions as unhinged. We don't spend twenty-three hours a day in sixty-square-foot cells with no TV, limited access to radio, books or magazines,

David R. Dow, "Life Without Parole: A Different Death Penalty," *The Nation* online, October 26, 2012. www.thenation.com. Copyright © 2012 The Nation. Reprinted with permission from the issue of The Nation. For subscription information, call 1-800-333-8536. Portions of each week's Nation magazine can be accessed at http://www.nation.com.

and no contact with other human beings (unless you count being escorted from point A to point B by often sadistic corrections officers). I've had clients who want me to fight for them, and then when we win and get their death sentence converted into life, end up telling me I've betrayed them.

Let me be clear: most of my clients want to live. Most of them prefer a life of virtually no freedom to no life at all. But underlying this preference is a hope, however faint, they might one day get out.

The Proposal to End Capital Punishment

On November 6 [2012], Californians will vote on Proposition 34, the Savings, Accountability and Full Enforcement (SAFE) for California Act. [The proposition was ultimately defeated.] The ballot initiative would abolish capital punishment in the state and replace it with a sentence of life in prison without the possibility of parole. Every week I get e-mails from national abolitionist groups touting the virtues of Prop 34. Facebook ads urge me to "like" it. But there are good reasons to believe that if the vote were up to the 725 inmates on California's death row, it would fail. When the Campaign to End the Death Penalty sent surveys on Prop 34 to more than 200 California death row prisoners, fifty inmates responded. Forty-seven opposed the measure.

Sending a prisoner to die behind bars with no hope of release is a sentence that denies the possibility of redemption every bit as much as strapping a murderer to the gurney and filling him with poison.

For California's 725 death row inmates, having their sentences commuted to life without parole would mean automatically losing their right to state-appointed lawyers to pursue their *habeas corpus* [right to appear in court] appeals. For a huge proportion, this would instantly rob them of every last ember of hope and increase by up to 20 percent the number of California inmates who will grow old and die behind bars. One California death row inmate recently wrote an op-ed opposing Prop 34 suggesting that he'd rather be executed than have his opportunities for appeal taken away. In a state that has executed only thirteen people since 1976, it would take two millennia to kill every current death row inmate, a fact that also helps explain how prisoners might oppose Prop 34.

Concerns over innocence seem to be at the heart of Prop 34. "California Leads the Nation in Wrongful Convictions," read a press release from the Yes on 34 campaign on October 24. "More Evidence that California Needs to Pass Prop 34 to Prevent Execution of an Innocent Person." Prop. 34 supporters point out that those with strong claims of innocence will still be entitled to receive court-appointed counsel. But few of the residents of death row will be able to make such a showing.

A Different Kind of Death Sentence

The justifications given by death penalty opponents who have embraced life without parole reveal the extent to which abolitionists have surrendered the moral basis of their position. It used to be that abolitionists argued that most people who commit bad acts can change and that the cruelest punishment one can inflict is to rob a human being of hope. But this concept—I hesitate to use the word "rehabilitation"—has seeped out of the criminal justice system over the past forty years. Prisons are now designed almost entirely for security in mind and not at all for socialization. Sentences have gotten steadily longer. And while states are turning away from the death penalty, they are replacing it with a different kind of death sentence. Sending a prisoner to die behind bars with no hope of release is a sentence that denies the possibility of redemption every bit as much as strapping a murderer to the gurney and filling him with poison.

Opponents of capital punishment often point out that the United States is the only developed Western country still executing prisoners, a comparison meant to shame us for being aligned with such human rights-violating countries as Iran, China and North Korea. It's not a bad argument, but exactly the same could be said about life without parole. Our neighbors to the south don't have it. Almost all of Europe rejects it. Even China and Pakistan, hardly exemplars of progressive criminal justice policy, allow prisoners serving life sentences to come up for parole after twenty-five years. Meanwhile, the United States imprisons wrongdoers for sentences that are five to seven times longer than sentences for comparable offenses in, say, Germany. Yet the recidivism rate in Germany is roughly 25 percent lower than ours.

There are scores, even hundreds [of prisoners], who could be released at no significant risk to society.

Abolitionists might say in response that there are plenty of other reasons to support life without parole over the death penalty. It is less expensive, for example. This is true; carrying out an execution costs at least twice as much—and perhaps five times as much—as sentencing a murderer to life without parole. The Yes on 34 campaign argues that the measure would represent $130 million per year in savings for California.

Combined with the innocence argument—undeniably effective in a nation rattled by 300 DNA exonerations—this strategy seems to be working. Last year, a Gallup poll recorded the lowest level of support for the death penalty in forty years. Compared to a decade ago, when juries sentenced 224 criminals to death in a year, in 2011 American juries sent seventy-eight people to death row, the first time since 1976 that new arrivals on death row dipped below 100. Even in Texas— especially in Texas—which became the last death penalty state to adopt life without parole, in 2005, the decline in death sentences has been precipitous. In 1999, Texas juries added forty-eight inmates to death row. Last year's number was eight.

The Need for Permanent Sentencing

There's no question that touting life without parole as the moral and cost-effective alternative to the death penalty has been a successful short-term strategy. But then what? Is it really necessary to eliminate any possibility of eventual release for all 725 people on California's death row? Charles Manson is not serving life without parole, but he has been rejected every single time he has appeared before the parole board and will die behind bars. Are some of California's death row inmates as monstrous as Manson? I suspect the answer is yes, and the parole board could keep them in prison too. But there are scores, even hundreds, who could be released at no significant risk to society.

We know this because it has happened before. When the Supreme Court briefly struck down the death penalty in 1972, 587 men (and two women) had their death sentences instantly converted to life, and more than half of them were eventually paroled. Of the more than 300 who got out, five committed another homicide.

That's five deaths too many, you might say, and I would not disagree. But that's not really the question. The question is whether we need permanent sentencing to prevent such crimes. The question is how much safer we are by having a punishment that forecloses on any possibility for redemption. The question is whether any marginal increase in safety and savings are justified by the high cost of keeping aging inmates behind bars until they die.

This series of questions, you might have noticed, is exactly the same as the set one might ask in the face of capital punishment.

The Death Penalty Should Be Abolished

Marc Hyden

Marc Hyden is the national advocacy coordinator for Conservatives Concerned About the Death Penalty, a project of Equal Justice USA.

On the evening of March 11, 2014, Glenn Ford was released from Louisiana's death row after 30 years of captivity for a murder that he did not commit. The prosecution had withheld testimony that would have exonerated Ford and relied on faulty forensic analyses. Unfortunately, Ford's story is not unique. It is one of many cases that exemplify the problems with today's death penalty system.

The Costs of the Death Penalty

Many states are grappling with the systemic dysfunction plaguing the current capital punishment regime, but they are finding it is difficult, if not impossible, to maintain such a program while reconciling its moral, pragmatic, and philosophical failures. The state ought not kill innocent citizens, but the death penalty carries an inherent and undeniable risk of doing precisely that. Whether through mistakes or abuse of power, innocent people routinely get sent to death row.

Some, like Ford, eventually get out: To date, 10 individuals in Louisiana and 144 nationally have been released from death row because they were wrongly convicted. Many others have been executed despite substantial doubts about the verdict.

The fiscal cost of the death penalty pales in comparison to the human cost, but local, state, and federal governments

Marc Hyden, "The Cost of Capital Punishment: Reconsidering the Death Penalty Is a Matter of Conscience and Constitutionality," *Freeman*, May 12, 2014. Copyright © 2014 by The Freeman. All rights reserved. Reproduced by permission.

must justify all spending as they struggle with ongoing budgetary shortfalls. John DeRosier, Louisiana District Attorney for Calcasieu Parish, estimated that a capital case in Louisiana is at least three times more costly than a non-death case. Studies in North Carolina, Maryland, California, and many others show that capital punishment is many times more expensive than life without parole, and there's a long history of the death penalty pushing municipal budgets to the brink of bankruptcy and even leading to tax increases.

Submitting the power to kill U.S. citizens to the State is unwise considering [the] history of error and malfeasance.

The fiscal impact of the death penalty is not lost on state governments. But they seem, broadly, more concerned with the fiscal impact than with the death part. Louisiana is currently considering House Bill 71, which is similar to Florida's "Timely Justice Act," which limits the appeals process. Had this legislation passed earlier, it would have likely led to numerous wrongful executions because it shortens the number of appeals available to death row inmates. Cutting the appeals process may, in the end, lead to modest cost savings, but the most expensive step in the death penalty process—pretrial activities and the actual trials—are unaffected by this legislation. And these are precisely the stages that produce wrongful convictions. Evidence proving them wrongful often emerges more than a decade after the initial trial, so the nominal savings are not worth the moral cost of executing an innocent person.

The Government's Ability to Take Life

The expense passed on to the taxpayers and risk of killing innocent people are often both justified by claims that the death penalty saves lives—it supposedly deters murder and provides the justice that murder victims' families deserve. Multiple scientific studies have actually shown that the death penalty doesn't deter murder. Many murder victims' family members are vocally rejecting this program because it retraumatizes them through a decades-long process of trials, appeals, and constant media attention.

There's no greater authority than the power to take life, and our government currently reserves the authority to kill the citizens it's supposed to serve. This is the same fallible government responsible for the Tuskegee Experiment, over-reach including NSA [National Security Agency] spying, and failures such as the Bay of Pigs. Of course, the death toll from wars government either started or intensified is staggering. Submitting the power to kill U.S. citizens to the State is un-wise considering this history of error and malfeasance.

And states aren't even complying with the standards that allegedly keep the death penalty from falling afoul of the "cruel and unusual" punishment standard.

The Need for Perfection

Many states can no longer obtain the previously used and ap-proved death penalty drugs. So they've started experimenting on inmates with new drug combinations acquired from secret sources. This has led to botched, torturous executions. In Ohio, Dennis McGwire audibly struggled for 25 minutes be-fore he died, and Clayton Lockett's execution in Oklahoma was postponed after he failed to die after 10 minutes. Indeed, Lockett only met his demise due to a heart attack, 30 minutes after the botched execution. Cruel and unusual?

Glenn Ford could have easily been subjected to the same experiences. Louisiana, like many other states, keeps the source of its death penalty drugs a secret. This secrecy calls into question the legality and validity of the drugs' manufacturers. We are far from the level of government transparency re-quired to limit government abuse, misuse, and power.

Most people will agree that the death penalty system is not perfect—but a program designed to kill guilty U.S. citizens *must* be perfect because the Constitution demands zero errors. To date, 18 states and the District of Columbia have abandoned capital punishment, aware that the system is broken and finally convinced, after years of legislative, judicial, and policy "fixes," that it cannot be mended. Other states still believe they can make capital punishment work properly, but they continue to break an already failed program one "fix" at a time.

Why Death-Penalty Opponents Can't Win

Jonah Goldberg

Jonah Goldberg is editor-at-large of National Review Online *and author of* The Tyranny of Clichés: How Liberals Cheat in the War of Ideas.

On Wednesday, two men were lawfully executed. Both insisted they were innocent. If you've been watching the news or following Kim Kardashian's tweets, you've likely heard of one of these men, Troy Davis.

The other death-penalty "victim," Lawrence Russell Brewer, was until this week the more significant convicted murderer. Brewer was one of the racist goons who infamously tied James Byrd to the back of their truck and dragged him to death in Texas.

The case became a touchstone in the 2000 presidential race because then-Texas governor George W. Bush had refused to sign a "hate crimes" law. The NAACP ran a reprehensible ad during the presidential election trying to insinuate that Bush somehow shared responsibility for the act.

Regardless, Brewer claimed that he was "innocent" because one of his buddies had cut Byrd's throat before they dragged his body around. Forensic evidence directly contradicted this.

Brewer's own statements didn't help either. Such as, "As far as any regrets, no, I have no regrets. . . . I'd do it all over again, to tell you the truth."

Brewer, festooned with tattoos depicting KKK symbols and burning crosses, was "not a sympathetic person" in the words of Gloria Rubac of the Texas Death Penalty Abolition Movement.

Jonah Goldberg, "Why Death-Penalty Opponents Can't Win," *National Review Online*, September 23, 2011. Copyright © 2011 by National Review. All rights reserved. Reproduced by permission.

Which is why we didn't hear much about him this week. Instead, we heard a great deal about Davis. Many people insist Davis was innocent or that there was "too much doubt" about his guilt to proceed with the execution. Many judges and public officials disagreed, including all nine members of the Supreme Court, who briefly stayed the execution Wednesday night, only to let it proceed hours later.

There is no transitive property that renders one heinous murderer less deserving of punishment simply because some other person was exonerated of murder.

There are many sincere and decent people—on both sides of the ideological spectrum—who are opposed to the death penalty. I consider it an honorable position, even though I disagree with it. I am 100 percent in favor of lawfully executing people who deserve the death penalty and 100 percent opposed to killing people who do not deserve it.

When I say that, many death-penalty opponents angrily respond that I'm missing the point. You can never be certain! Troy Davis proves that!

But he proves no such thing. At best, his case proves that you can't be certain about Davis. You most certainly can be certain about other murderers. If the horrible happens and we learn that Davis really was not guilty, that will be a heart-wrenching revelation. It will cast a negative light on the death penalty, on the Georgia criminal-justice system, and on America.

But you know what it won't do? It won't render Lawrence Russell Brewer one iota less guilty or less deserving of the death penalty. Opponents of capital punishment are extremely selective about the cases they make into public crusades. Strategically, that's smart; you don't want to lead your argument with "unsympathetic persons." But logically, it's problematic. There is no transitive property that renders one heinous murderer less deserving of punishment simply because some other person was exonerated of murder.

Timothy McVeigh killed 168 people including 19 children. He admitted it. How does doubt in Troy Davis's case make McVeigh less deserving of death?

We hear so much about the innocent people who've gotten off death row—thank God—because of new DNA techniques. We hear very little about the criminals who've had their guilt confirmed by the same techniques (or who've declined DNA testing because they know it will remove all doubt). Death-penalty opponents are less eager to debate such cases because they want to delegitimize "the system."

And to be fair, I think this logic cuts against one of the death penalty's greatest rationalizations as well: deterrence. I do believe there's a deterrence effect from the death penalty. But I don't think that's anything more than an ancillary benefit of capital punishment. It's unjust to kill a person simply to send a message to other people who've yet to commit a crime. It is just to execute a person who deserves to be executed.

Opponents of the death penalty believe that no one deserves to be executed. Again, it's an honorable position, but a difficult one to defend politically in a country where the death penalty is popular. So they spend all of their energy cherrypicking cases, gumming up the legal system, and talking about "uncertainty."

That's fine. But until they can explain why we shouldn't have a death penalty when uncertainty isn't an issue—i.e., why McVeigh and Brewer should live—they'll never win the real argument.

Getting Rid of the Death Penalty Would Eliminate Plea Bargains

Debra J. Saunders

Debra J. Saunders is a syndicated columnist for the San Francisco Chronicle.

Recently, editorial page editor John Diaz asked Mark Klaas whether he expects to feel closure if California executes Richard Allen Davis, the man who kidnapped, toyed with and then killed Klaas' 12-year-old daughter, Polly, in 1993. A jury found Davis guilty and sentenced him to death in 1996.

From the early days after Davis snatched Polly from a Petaluma slumber party, Klaas has been a highly visible advocate for strong laws to protect the public, especially children, from career criminals and predators like Davis. He had come to the *San Francisco Chronicle* with other opponents of Proposition 34, the ballot measure that would end California's death penalty and resentence California's 700-plus death row inmates to life without parole.

Klaas' answer may surprise you. He sadly shook his head and answered. "Is it going to bring any closure to me? No."

But, Klaas added, Davis "will no longer be able to run his website." Young girls no longer will write to him.

The Movement to End the Death Penalty

It turns out the Canadian Coalition Against the Death Penalty hosts a Richard Allen Davis home page, on which the convicted killer displays "hand-painted wood hobby craft items," which he made, and posts photos of himself. Davis also won-

Debra J. Saunders, "Get Rid of the Death Penalty, Get Rid of Plea Bargains," Creators .com, 2012. Copyright © 2012 by Creators Syndicate. All rights reserved. Reproduced by permission.

ders whether there's anyone out there who wants to know who he really is, and he asks, "For someone like myself, can one ever fall back in love with life again?"

Davis invites interested parties to write to him at San Quentin.

Klaas wants to see Davis executed, he told me later, because the man who killed his daughter should have no influence in this world. That, he emphasized, is "what's supposed to stop."

Good luck with that. Thanks to a highly successful defense lobby and federal judges who have stalled the enforcement of California law, only 13 of the state's death row inmates have been executed since 1992.

So now the folks behind Proposition 34 argue that California's death penalty is "too costly" and "broken beyond repair." End the death penalty, they say, and Californians will save money on sentencing trials, costly appeals and "special death row housing."

The anti-death penalty lobby is asking Californians to disarm themselves unilaterally.

The nonpartisan Legislative Analyst's Office estimates that the savings could amount to $100 million annually in the first few years.

There's a caveat with that number.

The Importance of Plea Bargains

The Legislative Analyst's Office also noted that it cannot compute the financial effect that might follow if murderers stopped pleading guilty and making plea bargains that enable them to avoid death row.

As Klaas sees it, the anti-death penalty lobby is asking Californians to disarm themselves unilaterally.

He cited cases like that of John Gardner. After the convicted sex offender was arrested for the murder of 17-year-old Chelsea King in 2010, Gardner went for a deal. He admitted to killing King and also to the 2009 murder and attempted rape of 14-year-old Amber Dubois. Gardner even led authorities to Amber's bones.

Parents Brent and Kelly King agreed to the plea bargain because, they said in a statement covered by CBS News, their family had been through "unthinkable hell" for 14 months. "We couldn't imagine the confession to Amber's murder never seeing the light of day, leaving an eternal question mark," they said.

"You take the death penalty off the table," Klaas told the *Chronicle*, and communities will be held hostage to the fear and uncertainty that follow when a young person goes missing. "Crimes will not be solved. Victims will not be recovered."

Without the death penalty, it is doubtful that Jared Lee Loughner would have pleaded guilty to a 2011 shooting in Tucson, Ariz., during which he killed six and wounded then-Rep. Gabrielle Giffords. Given his history of mental illness, it's not clear whether Loughner would have been found guilty.

The Need for the Death Penalty

Even when it doesn't work, the death penalty works.

California prosecutors and California juries do not reach the death penalty lightly. Sacramento Deputy District Attorney Anne Marie Schubert estimates that death row inmates represent less than 2 percent of those convicted for murder.

At least with the death penalty on the books, there's a good chance that some of the worst offenders will agree to a sentence of life without parole in order to avoid lethal injection.

In such cases, there is quick resolution and certainty of outcome, and victims' families need not worry about an offender's getting off, because the defendant has no grounds for appeals. All of the outcomes that the anti-death penalty lobby extols—cheaper, faster and more certain—exist only because of the death penalty.

Why would Californians want to get rid of it?

Organizations to Contact

The editors have compiled the following list of organizations concerned with the issues debated in this book. The descriptions are derived from materials provided by the organizations. All have publications or information available for interested readers. The list was compiled on the date of publication of the present volume; names, addresses, phone and fax numbers, and e-mail and Internet addresses may change. Be aware that many organizations take several weeks or longer to respond to inquiries, so allow as much time as possible.

American Civil Liberties Union (ACLU)
125 Broad St., 18th Floor, New York, NY   10004
(212) 549-2500 • fax: (212) 549-2646
e-mail: aclu@aclu.org
website: www.aclu.org

The American Civil Liberties Union (ACLU) believes that capital punishment violates the US Constitution's ban on cruel and unusual punishment as well as the requirements of due process and equal protection under the law. The ACLU Capital Punishment Project (CPP) works to abolish the death penalty nationally through direct representation as well as through strategic litigation, advocacy, public education, and mentoring and training programs for capital defense teams. The ACLU publishes numerous papers on the topic, including "The Case Against the Death Penalty."

Amnesty International USA
5 Penn Plaza, New York, NY   10001
(212) 807-8400 • fax: (212) 627-1451
e-mail: aimember@aiusa.org
website: www.amnestyusa.org

Amnesty International USA's Abolish the Death Penalty campaign seeks the abolishment of the death penalty worldwide. Its most recent activities have been aimed at decreasing the use of the death penalty internationally, including in the United States, and increasing the number of countries that have removed the death penalty as an option for punishment. It also serves as an advocate in individual clemency cases. Amnesty International USA publishes news, fact sheets, and reports, including "Death Sentences and Executions 2013," which are available on its website.

Campaign to End the Death Penalty (CEDP)
PO Box 25730, Chicago, IL   60625
(773) 955-4841
website: www.nodeathpenalty.org

The Campaign to End the Death Penalty (CEDP) is a national grassroots organization dedicated to the abolition of capital punishment in the United States. CEDP is involved in death row cases, does research and outreach, and protests executions. CEDP publishes updates on death row cases, fact sheets about capital punishment in the United States, and a newsletter, *The New Abolitionist*.

Crime Prevention Research Center (CPRC)
212 Lafayette Ave., Swarthmore, PA   19081
e-mail: info@crimeresearch.org
website: www.crimepreventionresearchcenter.org

The Crime Prevention Research Center (CPRC) is a research and education organization dedicated to conducting academic quality research on the relationship between laws regulating the ownership or use of guns, crime, and public safety. CPRC aims to educate the public and policy makers and takes a stand in favor of the death penalty. CPRC publishes numerous articles available at its website, including "What Does the Research on the Death Penalty Actually Show?"

Criminal Justice Legal Foundation (CJLF)
2131 L St., Sacramento, CA   95816
(916) 446-0345
website: www.cjlf.org

The Criminal Justice Legal Foundation (CJLF) was established in 1982 as a nonprofit, public interest law organization dedicated to restoring a balance between the rights of crime victims and the criminally accused. CJLF works to encourage precedent-setting decisions that recognize the constitutional rights of victims and law-abiding society and enable the deterrent effect of swift and decisive criminal justice. CJLF sponsors the blog *Crime & Consequences*, and its website offers links to various transcripts, articles, and working papers, including "The Death Penalty and Plea Bargaining to Life Sentences."

Death Penalty Information Center (DPIC)

1015 18th St. NW, Suite 704, Washington, DC   20036
(202) 289-2275 • fax: (202) 289-7336
e-mail: dpic@deathpenaltyinfo.org
website: www.deathpenaltyinfo.org

The Death Penalty Information Center (DPIC) is a nonprofit organization that provides the media and public with information concerning capital punishment. DPIC opposes the death penalty because it believes that capital punishment is discriminatory, costly to taxpayers, and may result in innocent persons being put to death. DPIC publishes reports and facts about the death penalty, as well as annual reports.

Justice for All (JFA)

PO Box 55159, Houston, TX   77255
(713) 935-9300
e-mail: info@jfa.net
website: www.jfa.net

Justice for All (JFA) is an all-volunteer, nonprofit criminal justice reform organization that supports the death penalty. JFA acts as an advocate for change in a criminal justice system that it believes is inadequate in protecting the lives and property of law-abiding citizens. It also provides links to stories about victims and information about the victims of death row inmates.

National Coalition to Abolish the Death Penalty

1620 L St. NW, Suite 250, Washington, DC   20036
(202) 331-4090
website: www.ncadp.org

The National Coalition to Abolish the Death Penalty's mission is to abolish the death penalty in the United States and support efforts to abolish the death penalty worldwide. The National Coalition to Abolish the Death Penalty works to repeal the death penalty state by state through strategic planning, campaign development, and training services. To further its goal, the Coalition publishes blogs, information packets, pamphlets, research materials, and the quarterly newsletter *Life-Lines*.

US Department of Justice (DOJ)

950 Pennsylvania Ave. NW, Washington, DC   20530-0001
(202) 514-2000
e-mail: AskDOJ@usdoj.gov
website: www.usdoj.gov

The mission of the US Department of Justice (DOJ) is to enforce the law and defend the interests of the United States according to the law. DOJ works to ensure public safety against foreign and domestic threats, to provide federal leadership in preventing and controlling crime, to seek just punishment for those guilty of unlawful behavior, and to ensure fair and impartial administration of justice for all Americans. Publications available on its website include annual capital punishment statistical tables as well as articles about current DOJ activities and links to DOJ agencies, such as the Civil Rights Division.

Bibliography

Books

John D. Bessler — *Cruel & Unusual: The American Death Penalty and the Founders' Eighth Amendment.* Boston: Northeastern University Press, 2012.

Robert M. Bohm — *Capital Punishment's Collateral Damage.* Durham, NC: Carolina Academic Press, 2013.

Raymond Bonner — *Anatomy of Injustice: A Murder Case Gone Wrong.* New York: Alfred A. Knopf, 2012.

Kathleen A. Cairns — *Proof of Guilt: Barbara Graham and the Politics of Executing Women in America.* Lincoln: University of Nebraska Press, 2013.

Martin Clancy and Tim O'Brien — *Murder at the Supreme Court: Lethal Crimes and Landmark Cases.* Amherst, NY: Prometheus Books, 2013.

David R. Dow — *The Autobiography of an Execution.* New York: Twelve, 2010.

David Garland — *Peculiar Institution: America's Death Penalty in an Age of Abolition.* Cambridge, MA: Belknap Press of Harvard University Press, 2010.

Brandon L. Garrett	*Convicting the Innocent: Where Criminal Prosecutions Go Wrong.* Cambridge, MA: Harvard University Press, 2011.
Bruce Jackson and Diane Christian	*In This Timeless Time: Living and Dying on Death Row in America.* Chapel Hill: University of North Carolina Press, 2012.
Richard S. Jaffe	*Quest for Justice: Defending the Damned.* Far Hills, NJ: New Horizon Press, 2012.
Charles Lane	*Stay of Execution: Saving the Death Penalty from Itself.* Lanham, MD: Rowman & Littlefield, 2010.
Eric Lose	*Living on Death Row.* El Paso, TX: LFB Scholarly Publishing, 2014.
Andrea D. Lyon	*Angel of Death Row: My Life as a Death Penalty Defense Lawyer.* New York: Kaplan Publishing, 2010.
Jen Marlowe and Martina Davis-Correia	*I Am Troy Davis.* Chicago: Haymarket Books, 2013.
David M. Oshinsky	*Capital Punishment on Trial*: Furman v. Georgia *and the Death Penalty in Modern America.* Lawrence: University Press of Kansas, 2010.
Louis J. Palmer Jr.	*The Death Penalty in the United States: A Complete Guide to Federal and State Laws.* Jefferson, NC: McFarland & Company, 2014.

Michael L. Perlin   *Mental Disability and the Death Penalty: The Shame of the States.* Lanham, MD: Rowman & Littlefield, 2013.

Wilbert Rideau   *In the Place of Justice: A Story of Punishment and Deliverance.* New York: Alfred A. Knopf, 2010.

James D. Slack   *Abortion, Execution, and the Consequences of Taking Life.* New Brunswick, NJ: Transaction Publishers, 2014.

Periodicals and Internet Sources

Allen Ault   "Ordering Death in Georgia Prisons," *Newsweek*, September 25, 2011. www.newsweek.com.

Marc Bookman   "The Confessions of Innocent Men," *Atlantic*, August 6, 2013.

Boston Globe   "New Hampshire Should Abolish Death Penalty," April 16, 2014.

Andrew Cohen   "The Problems with the Death Penalty Are Already Crystal Clear," *Atlantic*, May 5, 2014.

Boer Deng and Dahlia Lithwick   "Liberal Guilt," *Slate*, May 9, 2014. www.slate.com.

Richard C. Dieter   "Struck By Lightning: The Continuing Arbitrariness of the Death Penalty Thirty-Five Years After Its Re-instatement in 1976," Death Penalty Information Center, July 2011. www.deathpenaltyinfo.org.

Matt Ford   "Can Europe End the Death Penalty
                         in America?," *Atlantic*, February 18,
                         2014.

Alex Gibney,   "Redford, Gibney, Sarandon: Why
Robert Redford,   Conservatives Should Oppose the
and Susan   Flawed Death Penalty, Too," *Salon*,
Sarandon   March 21, 2014. www.salon.com.

Stephen John   "5 Things You Should Know About
Hartnett   the History of the Death Penalty,"
                         AlterNet, April 15, 2013.
                         www.alternet.org.

Richard Kim   "The Oklahoma Way of Death,"
                         Nation, May 26, 2014.

Pema Levy   "An Unlikely Conservative Cause:
                         Abolish the Death Penalty,"
                         Newsweek, May 14, 2014.
                         www.newsweek.com.

Tanya Lewis   "Why Lethal Injection Drugs Don't
                         Always Work as Expected," *Huffington
                         Post*, May 1, 2014.
                         www.huffingtonpost.com.

Dahlia Lithwick   "When the Death Penalty Turns into
                         Torture," *Slate*, April 30, 2014.
                         www.slate.com.

John R. Lott Jr.   "Another Round in the
                         Death-Penalty Debate," *National
                         Review Online*, May 13, 2014.
                         www.nationalreview.com.

Matt McCarthy   "What's the Best Way to Execute
                         Someone?," *Slate*, March 27, 2014.
                         www.slate.com.

Laura Moye | "Supreme Court Must Not Allow Executions of the Mentally Impaired," CNN, August 8, 2012. www.cnn.com.

New York Times | "State-Sponsored Horror in Oklahoma," April 30, 2014.

Leon Neyfakh | "The Conservative Case Against the Death Penalty," *Boston Globe*, May 25, 2014.

Marvin Olasky | "Better Off Dead?: Capital Punishment Versus (a Horrifying) Life Without Parole," *Townhall*, October 15, 2013. www.townhall.com.

Debra J. Saunders | "If Lethal Injection Is Torture, Who's Responsible?," *Townhall*, May 2, 2014. www.townhall.com.

Liliana Segura | "Florida's Gruesome Execution Theater," *Washington Post*, March 19, 2014.

Peter Singer | "The Death Penalty—Again," *Project Syndicate*, October 12, 2011. www.project-syndicate.org.

Jacob Sullum | "A Lethal Injection of Reality," *Reason*, May 7, 2014. www.reason.com.

Mark Tooley | "Jesus and the Death Penalty," *American Spectator*, May 3, 2014.

David Von Drehle "More Innocent People on Death
Row than Estimated," *Time*, April 28,
2014.

Paul Waldman "Where the Death Penalty Stands,"
American Prospect, April 18, 2014.

Lane Wallace "Are All Murderers Mentally Ill?,"
Atlantic, December 3, 2010.

Index

A

Abu-Jamal, Mumia, 51
African Americans, 59, 63, 88, 121
American Bar Association, 60, 63
American Civil Liberties Union (ACLU), 63
Asia, 37
Australia, 37, 49

B

Baime, David, 94
Baldus, David C., 91–92
Baldus Georgia study, 91–92
Baldwin, James, 105
Balko, Radley, 39, 68–75
Bateman, Christopher (Kip), 45–46
Belton, Delbert, 50
Berry, Wendell, 61
Bilbo, Theodore, 104
Bite-mark matching, 72
Blackstone, William, 61
Blecker, Robert, 21–25, 70
Blood-type matching, 72
Brewer, Lawrence Russell, 135, 136, 137
Buckley, William F., 105
Bush, George W., 135
Bushman, Brad, 60–67

C

California Commission on the Fair Administration of Justice, 78
Cambridge Union Society, 105
Campaign to End the Death Penalty, 127
Camus, Albert, 42
Canada, 37, 40
Canadian Coalition Against the Death Penalty, 138
Capital punishment. *See* Death penalty
Capital Punishment Clinic, 106
China, 37, 67, 129
Christians and the death penalty
  biblical teachings, 31–32
  opposition to, 33–34
  overview, 31
  problems over, 33
  support for, 34–35
Clark, Joseph Lewis, 64
Clinton, Bill, 55
Coates, Ta-Nehisi, 102–105
Cohen, Andrew, 53
Connecticut Study (2003), 94, 96
Cooke, Charles C.W., 39–42
Criminal justice and mental illness, 106–109
Criminal justice system reform, 74–75
Cruel and unusual punishment, concerns, 63–66

D

Davis, Allen Lee, 64–65
Davis, Richard Allen, 138–139
Davis, Troy, 99–101, 135–136
The Death of Punishment (Blecker), 21–25